FROM CRISIS
TO TRANQUILITY

FROM CRISIS TO TRANQUILITY

A Guide To Classroom: Management Organization and Discipline

SARAH M. ROBINSON, M.Ed

From Crisis To Tranquility

Copyright © 2021 by Sarah Robinson. All rights reserved.

No part of this publication may be reproduced, stored in a retrieval system or transmitted in any way by any means, electronic, mechanical, photocopy, recording or otherwise without the prior permission of the author except as provided by USA copyright law.

The opinions expressed by the author are not necessarily those of URLink Print and Media.

1603 Capitol Ave., Suite 310 Cheyenne, Wyoming USA 82001
1-888-980-6523 | admin@urlinkpublishing.com

URLink Print and Media is committed to excellence in the publishing industry.

Book design copyright © 2021 by URLink Print and Media. All rights reserved.

Published in the United States of America

Library of Congress Control Number: 2021920297
ISBN 978-1-64753-988-7 (Paperback)
ISBN 978-1-64753-989-4 (Hardback)
ISBN 978-1-64753-990-0 (Digital)

20.05.21

TABLE OF CONTENTS

About the Author 7
Dedication 9
Foreword 11
Chapter 1 - Introduction 13
Chapter 2 - Causes Of Discipline Problems 18
Chapter 3 - Classroom Management And Organization 26
Chapter 4 - Bullies And Troubled Kids Who Are They
    And What Do We Do Now 36
Chapter 5 - Promoting Good Behavior Discipline Techniques 59
Chapter 6 - Administration Co - Workers 84
Chapter 7 - Parents 88
Chapter 8 - Possible Problems/Solutions 97
Chapter 9 - Parent Involvement – Start Early 114
Chapter 10 - Summary 118
Chapter 11 - Useable Forms And Ideas 121
Chapter 12 - A Workshop For Parent's And Parental
    Involvement 176
References for parents 201
Bibliography 203

ABOUT THE AUTHOR

Sarah has been in the field of education for the past twenty-three years, beginning her teaching career in a small Catholic High School, with the responsibility of teaching 4 different grade levels; 9-12. Following that experience she took a position as Pre-K Principal with a diverse student population. Once she completed her leadership position, Sarah went back into the classroom to continue her teaching career. Her educational career includes teaching at the elementary, middle school, and high school level and is currently a lead teacher for a toddler program.

She brings to the writing of this manuscript the experience of working with students of various cultures, abilities, economic backgrounds and diverse home environments.

Sarah has completed her Bachelor's Degree in education and Master's Degree in Curriculum/Educational leadership. Having worked with students in various academic settings and of different language backgrounds, she brings an updated and current perspective of education. In addition, she brings an enthusiasm for teaching in an environment that is conducive to classroom learning.

It is the hope that the information presented in the following chapters will be beneficial and current for all educators who choose to read it.

The author feels, that in today's society, with classroom shootings, teacher harassment and students in crisis that the material can be a very valuable tool for all educators and those choosing to become educators.

DEDICATION

For my dearest and best friend in the world who inspired my writing and never gave up on me. Thank you, Glyn Money.

FOREWORD

There have been numerous books published regarding the topic of school discipline, classroom organization and student behavior. All have much to contribute to successful techniques in the areas listed. We as authors hope that the ideas presented here will enable administrators, student and classroom teachers' numerous methods and techniques of discipline, organization, understanding the uniqueness of the student as well as a view of student behavioral problems. A given method may work very well for one educator and be disastrous for another.

Why do we have classroom disruptions, including shootings at an alarming rate? One reason could very well be that students feel left out, picked on by other students or simply lost in the daily shuffle and have no means to express their feelings and deep-seated personal hurt.

This book is written and designed for the classroom teacher at any level, as the basic concepts of discipline, organization and student behavior do not necessarily differ from one grade level to another. They may, however, vary somewhat depending upon the age of the child.

It is the author's intent not to reinvent the wheel, but rather to put down, in a somewhat organized way, the ideas that have been found to work with students over the years and in a wide range of classroom settings.

When the elements discussed in this text is properly maintained teaching becomes much less strenuous. Therefore, teachers do not leave the classroom at the end of the day feeling" burnout" as they have been able to spend the majority of their energy teaching and having students involved in the learning process. We all realize that when we enjoy and have fun doing something the time and effort that it takes to accomplish a task seems minimal.

This text then was developed as a result of working with teachers, administrators, and parents over a wide range of grade levels. It is intended to serve as a daily guide for those working in the educational setting and that can be effective to those who use it, whether they are a college student preparing for a career in teaching, a first year teacher or a master teacher.

The author bringa to the text methods of effective discipline and classroom management from the perspective of almost thirty years of educational background and the most current college philosophies.

I wish to express my sincere thanks to each educator who has helped in some way to contribute to this text and the opportunity to have a father-daughter partnership in the writing and editing of this manuscript.

It is my belief that the material contained within the pages that follow can be extremely beneficial to <u>student teachers, teachers, administrators and parent volunteers</u> . Another use for the material is that of developing educational workshops for both parents and teachers.

CHAPTER ONE

INTRODUCTION

Student behavior problems are as old as formal education and the classroom setting. Following a few practical guidelines and applying basic principles of classroom organization as well as good common-sense educators can effectively handle most discipline problems. These may include getting to know your students, knowing the facts relative to an infraction, being knowledgeable of the rules that apply and knowing the correct time to take action. Most of all a teacher must have a "love relationship" in dealing with students even though at times it may seem impossible or unrealistic. Most students react in a manner in which they are approached.

It is extremely important that teachers have a one - hundred percent commitment to what they say. Too often we say things before determining the outcome of what a statement can create. We must set the standards and live up to them ourselves. When this takes place, we can expect the student to follow the examples we have set for them.

All behavior, whether constructive or destructive, has an underlying cause and affect. Educators do not often have the time or background to engage in a detailed psychological background of each student. The teacher must fulfill a complex role of parent, helper, enforcer and referee. We must teach children alternate ways of getting what they want. Although this task seems monumental, it is not when achieved in a reasonable balance manner. It then produces a learning environment that is less stressful for the teacher and gives ownership to appropriate discipline to the student.

RESTRAINTS

In our social system people are unsure of the restraints under which they are expected to work. This is true for the educator as well as the student. Appropriate behavior patterns thus emerge through a testing pattern: teachers with administrators and students with the teacher in the classroom. Recognition is paramount and as teachers we can understand that process when we deal with our co-workers and school administrators.

This is also true with students as they interact with their peers, teachers, counselors and administrators. To find this balance is one of the most important aspects in developing good discipline.

Almost weekly, on the National News and talk shows there is a segment on schools and student behavior, bullying, shootings and all that is wrong with the educational system. All this attention does not solve the problem of what is wrong with schools and student attitude. The solution lies with the educator and parent.

FOUR IMPORTANT FACTORS

There are four important factors in good classroom discipline. The first is to have an understanding of why children cause discipline problems in the educational setting. We will look at this with the hope that it will provide insight to many of the discipline problems that are faced each day by the classroom teacher. The second factor is the physical environment of the classroom setting. A room that is decorated with creative and interesting ideas thought provoking bulletin boards well lighted and physically arranged can reduce greatly the number of problems that transpire. The third is learning to develop good classroom management skills. These skills when exercised on a consistent basis will provide an environment that will reduce many of the daily problems of discipline. Lastly, but equally as important, is the instructional factor. Varying teaching methods, getting students involved in planning and creating ownership in the learning process can be the single most important process for continued and effective classroom discipline.

In this book we will look at these questions and hopefully try to develop answers that will be instrumental in providing help to an organized, well-disciplined classroom that the teacher, as well as the student, can enjoy on a daily basis.

WHAT IS GOOD DISCIPLINE

What is good discipline? How can we effectively work with and gain the support of the school administration in the discipline process? What is effective classroom management and how do we achieve this goal? What role do other teachers' in the school environment play in individual classroom discipline? How can we achieve a school wide plan to reduce the effort needed on the part of each individual in having effective discipline? What role does the student play in classroom discipline and organization? Are parents important in the discipline process and how do we enlist their support and partnership? How important is a " list " of rules in the classroom? Do they help or hinder the learning and effective discipline process? Why is consistency so important? Are students responsible for their actions or are they a product of their environment? What about the underachiever and the over achiever? How important is it that the teacher be the role model for the student? How do teaching techniques affect classroom behavior?

Although the questions are many, numerous times the solutions are easier than one wishes to realize and can be accomplished through the use of patience, love, understanding, and consistency in the way we react as the adult role model for our students.

How can we react with parents, co-workers and administrators in achieving the goals of effective classroom discipline? We will take a look at some basic behavioral problems and possible solutions that may be helpful to the classroom teacher on a daily basis.

It is basic good discipline to be able to motivate the student, provide ownership for every student just within their classroom, not just the leaders, be consistent and be aware of the discipline strategies that are bound to fail.

THE STUDENT

When reading the material provided keep in mind the following:
- A student is not an interruption of your work, but the purpose of it.
- A student is not a cold statistic - she/he is flesh and blood, a human being with feelings and emotions like your own.
- A student is not someone to argue or match wits with.
- A student is deserving of the most courteous and attentive treatment you can give.
- A student needs and seeks understanding from the classroom teacher, fellow students and the world around them.
- Each student's ability will be different from his or her classmates and the rate of productivity may vary from one student to another.
- A student's culture, family background, and educational interest may well differ from the classmate that is setting next to them.
- A student is the most important part of your business - not an outsider.
- A student needs to know that we as educators are human beings with feelings, needs, and goals.
- A student may come from a home environment that is in constant turmoil or one that does not allow for the proper form of communication, thus they may not release their frustrations and tensions in a satisfactory manner. The school may be the only safe zone for this student.

SUMMARY

Education can be a rewarding and exciting profession when the teacher can walk into the classroom each day and impart the knowledge that they have worked so hard and long to obtain and when students are motivated and responsive to the learning process. Discipline is the key to this goal.

CHAPTER TWO
―

CAUSES OF DISCIPLINE PROBLEMS

BASIC CHARACTERISTICS

Some knowledge of basic characteristics of students will be helpful when looking at the causes or reasons for students that create discipline problems in the classroom or another educational setting; i.e. field trips, the playground and in school assemblies.

In general the following characteristics are often present.

1. The student is insecure and will need to improve their self-esteem.
2. The student is unhappy with the classroom setting. He/she may be educationally unchallenged or over challenged by the material being presented or demands made. They may find themselves placed in a situation where they must deal with an individual that they do no understand or a strong personality conflict.
3. The student may have a short attention span and will need exercises to increase that attention span. A modification in the teaching techniques used by the instructor may be helpful.
4. The student is quick to anger due to problems existing outside of the educational setting.

5. The student may have an abnormal fear of failure due to past experiences.
6. The student lacks motivation to achieve.
7. The student is two or three grade level above or below the classroom mean instructional level.
8. The student tries to bully younger or smaller children in order to attain a level of superiority that they have not been able to achieve in a "normal and acceptable " manner.
9. The student may have a health problem that may not been addressed or diagnosed.
10. The student is hyperactive, due to medical problems.
11. A students association with other students who have a tendency to be a discipline problem because of cultural or economic background.
12. A student has a change in behavior from positive to negative.
13. The student refuses individual help when offered by the teacher or classroom assistant.
14. The student refuses to complete assignments.
15. The student argues with the teacher frequently, with no apparent reason.

It is not to be implied however, that the student must demonstrate each of these characteristics to be a discipline problem. A discipline problem can arise out of each one; therefore the teacher should be aware of the signs that may lead to conflict and a discipline query.

Recognizing the student who causes discipline problems in the classroom is the first step in solving or finding a resolution to negative behavior. As educators we must look at the children with understanding and perception. As a mechanic looks, listens and uses diagnostic tools that are available to him when fixing a car, so too must the teacher in dealing with children with discipline problems. We must first see if we can determine the cause before it can be altered. In doing so, we need to address the issue and obtain help from parents, administration, former teachers, and school specialists.

TYPES OF PROBLEMS

PHYSICAL PROBLEMS

Physical problems often times are present in children and the teacher is unaware of them due to lack of communication on the part of the school or family. Students with physical problems many times do not wish their parents/guardians to inform the school as they feel other children will become aware of the problem and thus make them **different** or stand out from their fellow classmates. The difficulty occurs more often in junior high and high school than in the elementary grades, as student peer pressure increases, as they grow older. Some of the physical problems that may be present are hearing loss (severe or partial); where the child does not hear or partially hears the instructions or presentation, and thus does not complete assignments or does inferior work. Vision problems are also present in some children with a student having partial sight, limited vision, or inversion of words and letters. Color blindness occurs in a number of cases as well.

A child may have had surgery, which has left him/her physically scarred, or may have body rashes, seizures, be a diabetic or any other number of physical problems. These problems can cause the child to react in a manner as to shield themselves from the other students, many times creating discipline problem, such as being a bully or being late for class.

MENTAL PROBLEMS

Sad to say many children come to school that are not capable mentally of being in the learning environment. The child may be withdrawn, have problems staying on task, and have outbursts of temper or a variety of other undesirable traits. The teacher, in this case, should contact the school counseling office as soon as possible for an evaluation of the child and receive help in handling the child if they are to remain in the classroom.

PSYCHOLOGICAL PROBLEMS

Psychological problems can be present in children from all cultures, economic settings and races. There are no boundaries on these problems when it comes to students. These problems can arise from a number of situations, both in school in society and in the home. As educators we have no way of knowing what the child endures when they are not in the school setting. Problems can arise from many situations to include, but not limited to divorce or sexual, physical and emotional abuse. This abuse is not limited to the home and can occur anywhere the child's environment takes them. The teacher when emphasizing the child's weakness or ridicules the child, not only hurts the child but often times does damage to the child that will last through their formal education process and beyond. A child suffering from these problems is often withdrawn, late for class, has difficulty relating to others including the teacher. In the later school years, students Sexual orientation, when different than the norm (although not a psychological problem), may manifest itself in the same manner.

GENERATION PROBLEMS

Many children suffer from what we sometime call a generation gap. They listen to their classmates as they discuss their family relationships. They feel left out as their parents or siblings may be much older or in some cases younger. It is difficult for the child to understand this and to understand the differences in the restrictions and expectations that are placed upon them.

One way of manifesting this concern or confusion is to act up in the classroom, thus receiving the attention that they may not get from siblings or parents. The teacher in the classroom may be the only source of recognition that the student has. All of us are aware that, by being noticed we obtain that needed recognition. Too often the student seeks that acknowledgment through negative behavior.

HOME PROBLEMS

It is difficult to address this cause of discipline as the reasons and causes can be so widely varied. Each student's situation can be so very distinct from any other student in the classroom. Students naturally protect their home environment and family members, as it is a rare case that the child is truthfully open to their teachers when the problems arise in the home.

The teachers should be aware that these problems can exist; especially when the student shows a tendency for being absent or late to school, does not want to leave at the end of the day, comes to school disheveled and has the ability to use foul or undesirable language. The teacher in this case cannot solve the problems for the student, however we can help the student work through them. We must be careful to approach the child privately keeping documentation in order to protect the child as well as the teacher. This documentation will be extremely helpful when it is necessary to work with other staff members or authorities.

The student will manifest their frustration regarding the dysfunctional family in many ways to include the lack of completing homework, careless work, be inattentive and withdrawn. The student may seek peer acceptance and attention to compensate for the lack of a proper home environment.

SCHOOL ENVIRONMENT

This area consists of a number of reasons of what may cause classroom discipline problems. We as educators often become so busy with our daily obligations that we are not aware of the school environment and how it may cause discipline problems.

Students react differently in different educational situations, one of which is a testing situation. Some students will handle the testing process with no problems; others will react by acting up due to their lack of prior achievement, fear of failure, and the response they will receive from their peers or family.

Working together with co-workers, so as not to allow one member of the faculty to set the standards for the classroom is essential for setting a positive school environment. This does not exclude any member of the teaching process, however it can and often causes discipline problems, as the student will work one teacher against the other. We have all heard student's reply that Mr. X allows this or that, and the coach said that I could participate.   All members of the faculty, no matter what their position, are an integral part of the teaching process, when there is a lack of a good communication and a collaborative effort on everyone's part the student will take advantage of the situation and use it to their respective advantage.

Social and racial problems occur more often in the school environment than we would like to admit. It is natural for students of the same economic, racial background to band together. When this occurs, it is a natural outcome that discipline problems will arise from this "banning together" in the classroom or school setting.

To avoid this we will discuss classroom organization and the need to provide instruction in cultural awareness, so as to allow all groups to share and feel proud about their cultures. This process can and will reduce friction between groups and reduce discipline problems in the classroom.

The school and the teacher have an obligation to develop usable units of instruction dealing with peer relationships, self -esteem, guidelines for co-workers, and the role of the administrator when dealing with school discipline.

No matter what the cause for the discipline problem, it can be addressed in a manner that will result in a solution of the problem. It is the author's opinion that the major cause of discipline problems is that the students need to be accepted by their family, peers and teachers. To achieve this goal is lofty but not impossible.

As educators, once we are aware of the cause of the problem it is much easier to address the issue and find solutions that are reasonable and acceptable to all individuals involved.

LEARNING PROBLEMS

Many of today's students, despite having adequate or above average intelligence, fail to produce acceptable academic work. They are frequently labeled in educational jargon as ' under- achievers" -- a term that denotes a discrepancy between a student's measured aptitude (I.Q. Score) and his/her actual day - to - day performance.

In a classroom setting, underachievers may exhibit a spectrum of behaviors -- ranging from complacency to overt resistance. A student may reject an assignment completely, or may instead engage in just a mechanical reading of the material.

Under-achievement is assumed to be prevalent in urban centers and among minorities. This assumption is not without some foundation. Social class does not necessarily determine school performance. Students from middle and high-income backgrounds are often among the under-achievers in a classroom. Other factors such as family attitudes, teacher expectations, unrealistic goals, peer pressure, a poor self-concept, or even a physical problem can often be significant.

We often classify these students as having <u>learning disabilities.</u> We should be aware and remember that a student classified with a learning disability does not necessarily have to have a low I.Q. to receive that classification.

A learning disability is a very complex and puzzling handicapping condition. It covers a very wide spectrum of varying characteristics and manifestations, which are often difficult to understand. It is this wide spectrum of characteristics that makes learning disabilities virtually "invisible "to untrained eyes.

As we look at the causes for behavior problems we can not exclude the student with learning disabilities and should be aware of some of the manifestations of learning disabilities which may be seen in the classroom.

Some of these are as follows:

1. Short Attention Span
2. Difficulty Following Directions
3. Trouble Vocalizing a Word
4. Unable to Discriminate
5. Poor Reading Ability or Comprehension
6. Poor Eye-hand Coordination
7. Difficulty in Sequencing
8. Disorganization
9. Difficulty Understanding Abstract Concepts
10. Poor Impulse Control
11. Directionally Difficulties
12. Angers Quickly
13. Indifference or Lack of Concern

SUMMARY

If a student exhibits a cluster of any of the above, he may have a learning disability. This disability more often than not will lead to discipline problems in the classroom if not addressed and modified by school personnel. Generally the teacher has the responsibility of assuming the major role and modification of behavior in this type of student.

CHAPTER THREE

CLASSROOM MANAGEMENT AND ORGANIZATION

INTRODUCTION

Classroom management and organization can be the most effective elements in reducing discipline problems in the classroom. This does not imply however, that discipline problems will not arise even in the most organized and well-managed classroom.

This chapter is designed to provide help to the beginning and veteran teacher as well as being an assistance to the substitute teacher with suggestions, and an explanation of some of the techniques that will be helpful in making the classroom environment one that will allow for the goals and objectives of the teacher to be accomplished with the help of the students in the classroom. Classroom management and its organizational skills can be effectively planned prior to entering the classroom on the first day of school. The implementation of this organizational plan and management process will provide for a well-run classroom with fewer discipline problems.

If you did not have the opportunity to develop a organizational and management plan prior to the beginning of the school year (the first day of school) it is never to late to stop and begin again.

Anticipate everything that can come up on the first day of the class. In case of a fire drill will you know how to lead the class out of the building? What is the bell schedule? Will you know when to expect the lunch bell and when it is dismissal time? In case a pupil needs the nurse, do you know where the nurse's office is?

Get to know the school plant. Locate the exits and staircases that your pupils will be expected to use. If you will need additional textbooks and supplies, where can you send for them? In case a child gets sick in the room, where can you get a custodial worker to clean up? If it rains on the first day os school, where will you pick up your class or what directions will you give your class for lunch?

If you spend quality time the first few weeks in the classroom, to develop your plan with the students it will pay dividends many times over. Time lost in disciplining cannot be devoted to the instructional process throughout the school year.

We know from research that students who have ownership and a responsibility to their learning process do much better academically and begin to require other students within the learning environment to assume responsibility for their own individual behaviors.

If you are a veteran teacher, have you dropped into time-wasting habits in the classroom? Are the first minutes of your classes boring to the students? Do students enter the classroom and waste the beginning minutes of the class not knowing what is expected of them on any given day? OR, Do you start briskly with business like procedures, the room cracking with interest ... with the promise of worthwhile and profitable class activities?

Are you unconsciously neglecting routine duties, the rules and procedures you have established for the classroom? OR, Are you considered to be one of the educational team that is reliable and effective in discipline and instructional practices?

If you are beginning teacher, are you inviting disaster at the start by using proven means of failure? OR, Are you the one in charge from the first minute class begins? Do you ask for trouble by attitudes and acts that dampen your students respect, good will towards you and the subject matter? OR, are you effective in setting the stage for learning and managing the day's production?

If you're a substitute teacher coming into a particular classroom are you familiar with the procedures of the classroom? If these are not available do you have a specific plan of your own that can be quickly provided to the students so as to eliminate any possible confusion on their part?

The questions that we need to ask ourselves from the first day of class and review periodically throughout the school year are two in number.

WHAT AM I DOING THAT I SHOULD NOT BE DOING?

WHAT AM I NOT DOING THAT I SHOULD BE DOING?

When we address organizational and management skills to include class rules and procedures, we are setting goals and standards for ourselves as well as the students. Setting standards for the classroom involves the creation of a positive learning environment and the establishment of good classroom discipline. Successful standards are quickly set when the educator brings a positive self-image to the classroom.

Every new classroom setting requires the immediate establishment of goals and procedures (rules) as the classroom management system must be based on these goals and procedures. We are constantly making decisions as educators, each of these decisions, large or small, effects classroom discipline. When making the decision throughout the school year we must apply the decisions to the goals, organization and management system we have established. If this is not done, the discipline process will not be consistent and we will find ourselves taking giant steps backwards in the process of good discipline.

Students need to understand and appreciate the limits of their classroom. There are limitations in respect to behavior, time, activities and even the physical space that is provided in the classroom or on the school campus as a whole.

In business one of the basic standards of operation is clarity of goals and it is the businessman's secret to success. Education is no different; it begins with the setting of standards, procedures and an organizational process that is workable for the teacher and students alike.

PLANNING AND ORGANIZATION

Planning and organization are critical in achieving good classroom management. The teacher as well as the students has a tendency to stay on task when planning is well thought out. Fewer discipline problems arise when student do not feel they have time to waste. Good planning also allows for time to be spent on educational activities that may not otherwise be accomplished due to time spent correcting and monitoring behavioral problems.

To indicate that one method of discipline is better than another is contrary to the authors experience and belief. Teachers, students and each learning situation can be totally unique. What works for one individual does not necessarily work for another. The school staff should agree on certain goals and procedures that may apply to the total discipline program for the school, thus eliminating the student's ability to work one individual educator against the other.

Teachers spend countless hours working with students who are disruptive in the classroom setting. As teachers we are generally left on our own to work through our classroom discipline problems, unless we are aggressive and self-confident enough to seek help from our co-workers. Often times when we do seek help it is to late and the classroom standards have already been set as well as the discipline problems that exist. It is extremely important and time that is well spent that the educator use the first few weeks developing goals, procedures and rules with the student. This process provides ownership for the student and leaves no doubt in the students mind what is acceptable or unacceptable.

CLASSROOM ORGANIZATION

Classroom organization can and is an effective tool in reducing discipline problems on a daily basis. Classroom organization for our purposes will deal with the actual physical layout and placement of items in the classroom.

We are all aware of situations that we have been in that are confusing, frustrating and lead us to indicate our displeasure to those around us. An example that we have all encountered is a shopping trip to the local supermarket. Have you ever taken notice of how the store is laid out, so as to lead you through items that you really did not need or had no intention of buying? What about the crowded checkout lines?

The classroom is no different. Take time at the beginning of the year or your first day of class to plan your classroom. Remove congested areas that will cause pushing, shoving near the classroom door. What about the location of a simple thing like a pencil sharpener? Is you classroom so arranged that students will not have to fall over each other to get to the sharpener or wastebasket? Are these items in your viewing range?

Seating arrangements are extremely important to effective classroom discipline. The instructor should seat students so that they are not facing the door or windows, thus eliminating the distractions that are occurring outside of your learning environment. If the classroom is designed in such a way the students must face the door that includes a window, cover the window with a poster. This reduces the number of times you well need to stop, comment or correct the student for not paying attention.

Student desks should be arranged in a manner that the blackboards, bulletin boards (when used for teaching) or any other instructional area are clearly visible to all of the students. When these arrangements are not planned out we are asking for discipline problems, as we require students to move about or lean over other students.

Classroom learning centers, experiment stations and the like should be located in such a way as to provide as little distraction, both visual and verbal, as possible to students seated in there desks.

Another "rule of thumb" is to arrange the classroom, including the teacher's desk in such a manner that you have easy access to all students in a very short period of time. Being able to move effortlessly about the room during class activities is not only important to the student but is an effective classroom management technique for the teacher.

When designing your classroom layout, it is important to keep these four key elements in mind.

1. Visibility
2. Accessibility
3. Distractibility
4. Proximity

A simple thing as the location of the wastebasket is an important element when planning to reduce classroom discipline problems. If items you need are not available it is important to work with the school administration in obtaining such items. Talking with the school administrator and giving your reasons for your requests is an essential part of the planning / classroom organizational process.

CLASSROOM MANAGEMENT - RULES

Although the authors do not believe in a great number of rules for the classroom, some are very necessary as they provide a foundation for what type of behavior is or is not acceptable behavior in the classroom.

Rules (objectives and procedures) are part of the classroom management system and must be taught just as you would teach any other subject matter. It is extremely important that the student knows the teacher's expectations, have ownership in the process, and realize the consequences that may occur when the objectives are not met and the procedures are not followed. The first few weeks in the classroom should be spent, with some time set aside each day, to teach the rules that have been developed in the planning stage. Consistency on the part of the educator is of extreme importance if the plan designed is to be effective and workable.

There are three basic elements in developing rules for the classroom. Each is equally as important as the others. They are as follows:

PLANNING IMPLEMENTATION AND MAINTENANCE

PLANNING

The first area that of planning is composed of the teacher developing a plan based on his/her goals and objectives for students and the classroom during a given school year.

When planning, a number of elements must be considered so that the plan is workable for the teacher as well as the student. These elements include the age level of the student, the philosophy of the school as a whole, the guidelines established by the administration and the background of the students themselves. When developing goals and procedures for the classroom the educator should remember that those goals and procedures are only as good as the educator's ability to enforce them.

In the planning stage the teacher will want to consider the use of space in the classroom, location and arrangement of desks, learning centers, lab centers, displays and any other item unique to the classroom setting. How do you wish this area to be used and what procedures are necessary to assure an orderly classroom environment? What procedures does the teacher wish to have for homework completion, for the use of rest rooms, use of pencil sharpener, wastebasket, completion of an assignment within the classroom setting? In each case the procedures designed may vary with the classroom, experience of the teacher, student population, school policies and student input. Procedures should be designed that develop responsibility and accountability on the part of each student.

The teacher can develop these procedures either alone or with a veteran teacher on the staff, however students need to be partners whenever possible, as this process does provide ownership for the student and will result in better discipline in the classroom as a whole.

When writing goals and procedures it is important that these goals and procedures be developed in a positive manner. For example, a procedure might be written as given in the following examples:

Please walk when entering the room, rather than <u>Don't Run</u>

We can allow one person to go to the rest room at a time, rather than - <u>No more than one person will go to the rest room at a time.</u>

Procedures when developed should also take into account that the students can be accountable for the procedures and work toward reaching the goals developed in the classroom.

IMPLEMENTATION

Now that you have developed the goals and procedures (rules) that you feel are important to your classroom, the second step is to work toward implementation of these procedures.

Students cannot and should not be expected to handle a great number of rules at any one time. The teacher should list for himself or herself in priority which rules are the most important in developing a good discipline strategy for their classroom and work on implementing the rules with the highest priority first.

The next step is to work, in a lesson or activity format, with the student in order to teach the specific procedure. The lesson or activity can be extended to the home, which would be very helpful, through a homework assignment. Students need to be aware of the reason for the procedure and also be aware of the outcomes if the procedures are not followed. Outcomes must be reasonable and the teacher needs to state them clearly. Consequences that are not enforceable have little or no value in the discipline process and often lead to greater discipline problems.

Students involved in the implementation stage of the management process, should be provided a model for each of the procedures that are going to be implemented. In doing so, the teacher creates an atmosphere of sharing and is assured of an understanding on the part of the individual student.

MAINTENANCE

The maintenance of the goals and procedures developed in the classroom should be addressed initially at the planning stage. If a maintenance plan is not developed and carried out in the classroom, the goals and procedures soon fall by the wayside and discipline problems begin to arise. We as educators become so busy with the daily requirements placed upon us by administration; developing good lesson plans, that we set aside the discipline process due to time restraints.

Be consistent in the maintenance process. Do not be afraid to change the procedures if they are not working for you. Teachers must find a balance and not be afraid of saying or sharing with the students that certain procedures may need to be modified after a period of time. Re-teach the classroom rules on a monthly or quarterly basis through constructive and creative lessons and activities. The time you spend on re-enforcing the rules will pay high dividends, quality use of time in the classroom, and the reduction of stress on the part of both the teacher and student.

Evaluate and revise the maintenance process based on the goals you have established, using positive reinforcement with the students.

SUMMARY

Although it may take time to develop an organization and management system for your classroom, it may very well be an extremely profitable endeavor, for if you can reduce the time you will need to spend on discipline. You will gain a classroom that is more enjoyable for you and the student, increase the time you are able to spend on quality instruction, see an improvement in academic levels of achievement and decrease your stress level. So often we see new teachers so excited about entering the classroom for the first time but then see them burn out after a few months. We also see veteran teachers wishing to give up the teaching profession due to the daily hassles of disciplining. Classroom organization and management is a way to reduce this frustration. It is not something that is not taught during the years of preparation in college, nor is it provided through quality in-service programs. Once the teacher enters the classroom, they are on his or her own. It is much easier to develop good organizational and management skills at the beginning than to try to re-due a difficult situation. It is possible to handle either by spending that needed time in planning, developing goals, procedures and teaching these elements to the students in the classroom.

Keep in mind the following:

1. Do not expect miracles overnight. " Rome wasn't built in a day".
2. Create simple small tasks that are highly structured with immediate reinforcement.
3. Stress student responsibility from the start.
4. Don't use threats. State requirements in terms of Consequences.
5. Do not accept excuses; show them you know
6. State your position clearly so they can succeed
7. Be consistent.
8. Have the students evaluate their behaviors during a class setting or in private with the teacher.
9. Keep on trying, be willing to change, plan Carefully

CHAPTER FOUR

BULLIES AND TROUBLED KIDS WHO ARE THEY AND WHAT DO WE DO NOW

In this section we will look at two different types of students. Why is this important? It seems as though it is becoming more and more frequent that our attention is being drawn by the news media to events that occur on school campuses across the United States where students are bring knifes, guns, threatening to bomb a school building or simply set the campus on fire. The authors feel that there is a direct relationship between this type of behavior and the student who is commonly classified as a bully or one who is being bullied by his

It is no surprise to educators that many students are bullied and many of them ask for it by their mannerisms however often times a variety of reasons exist for both the student who is the bully and the student who is bullied. We cannot ignore the troubled kid and hope the problem will go away, or at least not exist in our classroom or setting.

Not all students are likely to be bullying behavior. Those students who are more prone to the target of the bully tend to have some common characteristics. As educators we should be aware of these traits and if we are we can avoid many problems before they become full blown and cause the student to react in a manner that is harmful to him or to others. Teachers from across the country have made important suggestions that can be very useful to all educators in their respective classrooms.

KNOW YOUR GOALS

"Promote a school wide anti-bully environment. Implement an anti bullying campaign that involves the entire school community: parents, students, teachers, and administrators. If the entire school level is not achieved let the classroom adopt individual policies against bullying. Discuss with your students what bullying is, identify bullying behaviors, and share personal stories and facts of bullying. Work with your students to develop classroom rules/policies against bullying. Post signs designating and supporting a "bully free" classroom." "The first goal of all schools and classrooms is the safety of the students. The second goal is the level of comfort a student feels in order to report any bullying. In the beginning, mid, and end of each year, administer a classroom survey to assess the problem of bullying. Share the results with your students and discuss solutions to any bullying problems that are identified in the survey. Instill, from the very beginning, a zero tolerance for bullying. It is important to instill this comfort level in the classroom and to respond to a report of bullying effectively from day one". **4th Grade Teacher: Rosebud, Montana**

THE POWER OF SUPERVISION

"Provide students with increased adult supervision at prime bullying opportunities such as lunch and recess. Implement clear expectations used by the staff to promote consistency in the daily interactions with students and their behaviors. Make sure everyone knows the expectations. When bullying occurs, call students to task immediately by separating them from the rest of the group." **Primary Grade Teacher: Hibbing, Minnesota**

HAVE A PLAN OF ACTION

"Describe and discuss with your students the types and kinds of bullies. You may want to find a book that deals with bullying and read excerpts to your students. After discussion takes place on the topic of bullying, specify a clear and effective plan to deal with a bullying situation, including consequences of the behavior. For your own purposes, indicate when to include an administrator, teacher, and parent. The students can also be involved in defining processes. Evaluate and revise the plan on a yearly basis" **6th Grade Teacher: Rockland, Maine**

EMPOWER YOUR STUDENTS

"Promote the welcoming of new students by demonstrating and role playing friendship skills. Provide various simulations for students to develop the necessary skills to deal with bullying situation, thus empowering students with conflict resolution and peer mediation skills. If you do not have this sort of background, then find a resource that can help you develop these skills in your students **Intermediate Grade Teacher**: Ramapo, New Jersey

To bring the importance of this across to the reader the authors have included an article broadcasted by ABC News on January 3, 2002. It states the following:

SERIOUS BULLYING

"Dangerously Underrated Problem May Be at Root of Shootings and Suicides"
(*ABC News.com- January 3, 2002*)

Nov. 28 — Authorities say a planned massacre at a New Bedford, Mass., high school could have been another Columbine — or perhaps even worse — if police hadn't gotten wind of a group of students' alleged plot to detonate explosives, shoot classmates, and then kill themselves.

The students have pleaded not guilty, but according to police reports, the five teens who allegedly planned the attack had complained of being picked on and called names. A note found by a janitor at the school spoke of "getting everyone back for calling us names and beating us with ugly sticks."

The statement is reminiscent of the suicide note left by Eric Harris, one of the two attackers at Columbine High School in Littleton, Colorado: "Your children who have ridiculed me, who have chosen not to accept me, who have treated me like I am not worth their time, are dead."

Experts say bullying is a serious and widespread problem that can lead to school shootings and suicide. At the same time, they say, it is dangerously underrated, as schools and adults are not taking the problem seriously enough.

"For the child who's been targeted by a bully, their life is a living hell," said Glenn Stutzky, a school violence specialist at Michigan State University. "Bullying is probably the most frequently occurring form of violence in American schools today and it's really the engine that's driving the majority of violence. It's a huge problem."

Even though several states have now passed anti-bullying legislation, Stutzky said the American school system is 10 to 15 years behind countries like Australia, Scandinavia, Great Britain and Japan, all of which deal with bullying as a serious social problem.

"We have allowed a culture of abuse to thrive unchecked in our nation's schools," said Stutzky, "and we are paying for it with the bodies of our children."

PHYSICAL AND EMOTIONAL TOLL

Though it seems so hard to understand the anger that would fuel children to plot a massacre at their high school, sadly, many children can relate to the feelings of loneliness, abuse or resentment.

"Once I got teased, I could see where that anger comes from and what can make someone want to kill," said Stefan Barone, a 14-year-old from Staten Island, N.Y., who said he was bullied during seventh and eighth grades. "Even though I never got to that point, I could understand where it was coming from."

Day after day throughout the country, kids wake up terrified to go to school, knowing they will be the victims of teasing, taunting, name calling or physical abuse.

For Rachel Fannon, 16, being abused by her classmates in Littleton, Colo., for 5 ½ years took both a physical and emotional toll.

"They had actually a contest: They'd high-five each other if they come up with the best name how to describe how ugly I was," she said. "They'd kick me in the back of the knees and give me small bruises or they tripped me."

Fannon, who has a heart condition, would suffer attacks of rapid heartbeats after being harassed. Her grades dropped. She became withdrawn and had no friends. After school she would lock herself in her room and cry.

"All day, every day, they kept harassing me," she said. "Everywhere I went, there they were."

Fannon said teachers told her to "tough it out" or to "just ignore it." She said she was too embarrassed to tell her parents, but she finally confided in her mother. Principals of her school say the complaints never reached them, but they admit that despite their anti-bullying policies, Fannon somehow fell through the cracks.

Fannon — who now goes to a new school where she says she is treated "like a human being" — is hardly alone.

Despite being 6 feet 11 inches and 280 pounds, Chris Velasquez, now 14, said he was beaten so badly at his middle school that one time he was taken to the emergency room.

"They caught me in the stairwell and jumped me and I couldn't see anything," he recalled. "I had one kid punching me a lot of times in the face, and one just repeatedly hitting me in the back."

Though the incident was reported to school authorities, Velasquez said the boys who beat him up were not even suspended. His family is now suing the school district.

"We have a whole generation of adults in the educational system that still view bullying, as 'just that's the way it is,'" said Stutzky. "It's a rite of passage, it's boys being boys ... stop whining about it, life is tough, you just have to put up with it and make your own way through."

POSSIBLE CONSEQUENCES: SCHOOL SHOOTINGS AND SUICIDE

To deal with being bullied, some children seek revenge. Velasquez can understand. "I do think about going into school and doing something," he said. "But then I think what will that make me look like? A criminal."

Other children turn their anger inward. Each year, one out of 13 kids under the age of 19 attempts suicide, a rate that has tripled over the last 20 years. Last year, more than 2,000 of them succeeded — a staggering number Stutzky blames largely on bullying.

"We're not even realizing the fact that suicide is bullring's quiet little secret," he said. "It's picking off our children one at a time."

Twelve-year-old Tempest Smith was one of them. From the time she was in the second grade, said her mother Danessa Smith, Tempest was the brunt of cruel jokes and constant humiliation.

One time, recalls Smith, a group of kids pretending to be Tempest's friends came over to her house, only to ransack her room. Tempest would also be pushed in the lunch line, and her classmates would purposely knock things off her desk.

Smith said the school wouldn't even acknowledge there was a problem. "If it was not done in front of them, there's nothing they could do," Smith said she was told.

By the time Tempest reached the seventh grade, Smith was so fed up that she planned to home-school her daughter. But she never got that chance. On Feb. 20, Tempest took her own life.

Smith is now suing the school district, which has denied any wrongdoing.

Though Tempest cannot benefit from her peer's advice, Stefan Barone wanted to share advice with others who feel isolated and alone: "I'd like to say that there's going to be an end to it sooner or later … One day it's going to end and everything's going to turn around … you have to have hope."

BULLYING IS COMMON

STUDY: APPROXIMATELY 30 PERCENT OF STUDENTS BULLY OR ARE BULLIED

By Amy Malick

B O S T O N, April 24 — Maybe you were the one who got slapped around. Or maybe you did the slapping. A new study says that, if you're a teen today, you're one of many who are on the giving or receiving end of bullying. And the younger teens have it worse.

Almost a third of teens, in fact, either are bullies or are bullied, a new study of 16,000 students found.

Researchers at the National Institute of Child Health and Human Development found that 30 percent of sixth- through 10th-graders are involved in bullying at school.

The frequency of bullying was found to be higher among sixth- to eighth-graders compared to ninth- and 10th-graders, and was more prominent among boys compared to girls.

The study, led by Dr. Tonja Nansel, analyzed surveys of almost 16,000 students throughout the United States and appears in the April 25 issue of *Journal of the American Medical Association.*

WHAT IS BULLYING?

Bullying was defined as when a teen's behavior is purposefully meant to harm or disturb another child, when it occurs repeatedly over time, and when there is an imbalance of power between the kids involved.

Types of bullying behaviors cited in the study included verbal belittling regarding religion, race, looks, or speech; hitting, pushing or slapping; spreading rumors; and making sexual comments or gestures.

The study also found that both the perpetrators and the victims are lonelier than most kids and do not have very good relationships with their peers.

"Bullying and being bullied appear to be important indicators that something is wrong, and children who experience either or both need help," said child psychology experts Dr. Howard Spivak of the New England Medical Center in Boston and Dr. Deborah Prothrow-Stith of the Harvard School of Public Health, commenting on the research.

ARE BULLYING AND LATER VIOLENCE LINKED?

In light of recent school shootings, parents and educators have become concerned about whether bullying behavior or being the victim of one may contribute to more serious acts of aggression.

But experts disagree about predicting future violent behavior from earlier bullying tendencies.

Dr. Robert Fondling, director of child and adolescent psychiatry at the University Hospital of Cleveland, believes "aggression is a very stable trait that is long-lasting."

Dr. Carl Bell, director of public and community psychiatry at the University of Illinois in Chicago, adds, "There is some link between bullying behavior and later violence, but we are just not certain how strong it is."

One commonly cited British study reported that individuals with a history of bullying had a fourfold increase in criminal behavior by the age of 24. The British study, however, examined only violent behaviors

— such as beating up someone after school, and not the more benign behaviors like name-calling or giving someone the cold shoulder.

But some see bullying as part of the more normal aspect of children's behavior, not leading to excessive violence later on.

Dr. Eugene Beresin, director of child and adolescent psychological training at McLean and Massachusetts General hospitals, says, "School shootings are an anomaly, over-rated, exaggerated, and extremely rare ... Bullying, however, is very common and has definite serious social effects ... We should be much more concerned with bullying and self-inflicted violence."

SECRET SERVICE QUESTIONS BULLYING IN SCHOOL SHOOTERS

In fact, when the Secret Service recently attempted to figure out the "profile" of a child who acts out with gun violence, it found a student's tendency to become a "school shooter" cannot be predicted based on involvement in bullying activities.

COMMON CHARACTERIZES OF STUDENTS WHO ARE BULLIED

Some of the more common characteristics (but by no means is this list complete) of the student who is on the receiving end of the actions of the bully are as follows.

- Low self esteem
- Being insecure
- Lack of social skills
- Enable to pick up on social cues
- Overweight or underweight
- Having a physical disability
- Having a learning disability
- Shy or loner types
- Students who lack personal hygiene

- Students who may be gay or lesbian
- Lack of proper clothing
- Cry or emotionally unstable
- Ashamed of their parents or siblings
- Abused at home, mentally or sexually

Some children actually seem to provoke their own victimization. These children will tease bullies; make them a target by egging the person on, not knowing when to stop and then not being able to effectively defend him or her when the balance of power shifts to the bully.

Children who are not bullied tend to have better social skills and conflict management skills. They are more willing to assert themselves about differences without being aggressive or confronting. They suggest compromises and alternate solutions. They tend to be more aware of people's feelings and are the children who can be most helpful in resolving disputes and assisting other children to get help.

Reactive victims straddle a fence of being a bully and or victim. They are often the most difficult to identify because at first glance they seem to be targets for other bullies. However, reactive victims often taunt bullies, and bully other people themselves. Most of the incidents are physical in nature. These victims are impulsive and react quickly to intentional and unintentional physical encounters. In some cases, reactive victims begin as victims and become bullies as they try to retaliate. A reactive victim will approach a person who has been bullying him/her and say something like, "You better not bug me today, otherwise I'll tell the teacher and boy, will you be in trouble, so you just better watch out." Statements such as this are akin to waving a red flag in front of a raging bull, and may provoke a bully into action. Reactive victims then fight back and claim self defense. Reactive victims need to learn how to avoid bullies.

WHO IS THE BULLY?

Bullying can take many forms: physical, emotional, verbal or a combination of any of these .It may involve one student bullying another, a group of children against a single child or groups against other groups (gangs). Bullies do not come from one social classification; they are spread across the socio-economic gamut. Sometimes bullying is so subtle that that teacher, school or victim does not realize that is occurring. There are a vast number of students who are controlled by those who portray to be their friends and accept this control so as not to be left out of the mainstream.

Other concerns schools should be aware of is that the vast majority of the students in school today are from homes where one or more of the parents are either not present, have divorced and remarried bring other siblings into the family circle, the number of times a child has moved from one school environment, one city to another. All of these factors allow for a student to be a victim of the bully.

The bully thrives when and is not unlike other forms of victimization and abuse in that if contains:
- An imbalance of power
- Differing emotional tones, the victim gets upset giving the bully the upper hand and control.
- Placing blame on the victim for a event or loss of a friend, boyfriend, girlfriend.
- Lack of concern of the victims feelings and concerns
- Lack of compassion

Bullies are often students who have been bullied or abused themselves. They often are unable to cope with life situations that leave them feeling alone, helpless and not in control. They could be students who have inadequate social skills, family problems, do not meet expectations of the family, classroom or social environment. Being a bully thus places them in control. It is fairly easy to spot the bully if we turn ourselves into listening to our students, groups as they converse with each other and observe those situations where one student is fearful or overly dependent upon another student.

KINDS OF BULLIES

Physical bullies are action-oriented. This type Of Bullying includes hitting or kicking the victim, or, taking or damaging the victim's property. This is the least Sophisticated type of bully; it is so easy to identify. The entire population in the school soon knows physical bullies. As they get older, their attacks usually become more aggressive. These aggressive characteristics manifest themselves, as bullies become adults.

Verbal bullies use words to hurt or humiliate another person. Verbal bullying includes name-calling, insulting, making racist comments and constant teasing. This type of bullying is the easiest to inflict on other children. It is quick and to the point. It can occur in the least amount of time available, and its effects can be more devastating in some ways than physical bullying because there are no visible scars.

Relational or relationship bullies try to convince their peers to exclude or reject a certain person or people and cut the victims off from their social connections. This type of bullying is linked to verbal bullying and usually occurs when children (most often girls) spread nasty rumors about others or exclude an ex-friend from the peer group. The most devastating effect with this type of bullying is the rejection by the peer group at a time when children most need their social connections.

Reactive victims straddle a fence of being a bully and or victim. They are often the most difficult to identify because at first glance they seem to be targets for other bullies. However, reactive victims often taunt bullies, and bully other people themselves. Most of the incidents are physical in nature. These victims are impulsive and react quickly to intentional and unintentional physical encounters. In some cases, reactive victims begin as victims and become bullies as they try to retaliate. A reactive victim will approach a person who has been bullying him/her and say something like, "You better not bug me today, otherwise I'll tell the teacher and boy, will you be in trouble, so you just better watch out." Statements such as this are akin to waving a red flag in front of a raging bull, and may provoke a bully into action. Reactive victims then fight back and claim self defense. Reactive victims need to learn how to avoid bullies.

Children exhibiting these types of behaviors could be considered classroom bullies.

- Picking on another student because the student is different,
- Using verbal or physical aggression on a student(s),
- Threatening other students,
- Calling another student names and ridiculing other students
- Lying to others about a particular student.
- Damaging the belongings of another student(s)
- Threatening to harm others unless something is done or given to avoid the harm

DEALING WITH CLASSROOM BULLIES

For teachers and administrators dealing with classroom bullies it should be kept in mind that you are dealing with the issue not matter how distasteful it may be to provide a safe and enjoyable learning environment for all the students in the school. Remember that the bully has had previous success or he would not be the bully that he/she is in your classroom.

It is essential to involve all elements of the student's contacts with the problem solving process. Teachers, parents, and students need to be involved. The teacher has the primary role in dealing with both the bully and the student who is being bullied. It cannot be said enough that attention must be paid to the student who is being bullied, for it is this student who often reacts in violent action against him/her self, the school or the community. Listening and being aware of the hurt will go a long way in accomplishing the healing process.

Parents although repeatedly said but not often achieved are an essential part of correcting the problem. Many parents will choose to ignore the fact that their child is a bully. By doing so they tend to think that the problem will disappear. In order to achieve a lasting solution, parents must be involved. See the section of this book on hints for working with parents.

Students need to be involved in dealing with bullies. Students will know much sooner who the bully is and what effect they have on other students and the school environment.

When it comes to discipline or punishment issues, most students strongly believe in fairness and therefore welcome Anti-Bullying policies that encourage treating others with care and respect. However, students are more likely to support an Anti-Bullying campaign when they have been directly involved in determining the need for such a program, and deciding on its implementation. This includes developing Anti-Bullying policies and subsequent school-wide or classroom activities. It is necessary for students to promote the concept that caring for others is a valued quality, one that they accept and encourage.

A major cause of stress at school for students is the fear of being taunted or bullied. Students who are bullied are two to three times more likely to have headaches or other illnesses. (ABC News, Sept. 22, 1996) Schools need to establish a social climate where physical aggression and bullying are not used to gain popularity, maintain group leadership or influence others to do what they are told to do. No one deserves to be bullied. Once the 60% of children who are neither victims nor bullies adopt the attitude that bullying is an unacceptable behavior, schools are well on their way to having a successful bullying program.

Schools need to advertise the fact that they have adopted a Zero Tolerance policy for bullying, and that they have a workingman-bullying plan in force. School faculty must maintain a high Profile in terms of the behavioral expectations of their students in order to gain support from the community and send a clear message to the families of present and future students that bullying will not be tolerated.

Once a school has established itself as a safe place for all students, school personnel will need to continually work at maintaining that reputation. It is a difficult task that requires the school faculty have student safety at the top of their priority list. Remember, students who do not feel safe at school are unlikely to perform as well academically as they are capable, thus possibly impeding their future opportunities. A commitment by the staff to no-bullying in the school must be a long term undertaking. When a new school year begins, staff should be sure Anti-Bullying policies have been included and discussed in the yearly goal setting process.

Schools can create support groups where victims can concentrate on developing the skills needed to change their place within the social hierarchy of the student body. The goal is for the victim to become a part of the group of students who do not bully and are not bullied. Such changes require a great deal of time and effort, but it is possible, given the necessary support. It will not be tolerated.

Once a school has established itself as a safe place for all Students, school personnel will need to continually work at maintaining that reputation. It is a difficult task that requires the school faculty to put student safety at the top of their priority list. Remember, students who do not feel safe at school are unlikely to perform as well academically as they are capable, thus possibly impeding their future opportunities. A commitment by the staff to no-bullying in the school must be a long term undertaking. When a new school year begins, staff should be sure Anti-Bullying policies have been included and discussed in the yearly goal setting process.

Schools can create support groups where victims can concentration developing the skills needed to change their place within the social hierarchy of the student body. The goal is for the victim to become a part of the group of students who do not bully and are not bullied. Such changes require a great deal of time and effort, but it is possible, given the necessary support. Will not be tolerated by the school..

Once a school has established itself as a safe place for all students, school personnel will need to continually work at maintaining that reputation. It is a difficult task that requires the school faculty to put student safety at the top of their priority list. Remember, students who do not feel safe at school are unlikely to perform as well academically as they are capable, thus possibly impeding their future opportunities. A commitment by the staff to no-bullying in the school must be a long-term undertaking. When a new school year begins, staff should be sure Anti-Bullying policies have been included and discussed in the yearly goal setting process.

Schools can create support groups where victims can Concentrate on developing the skills needed to change their place within the social hierarchy of the student body. The goal is for the victim to become a part of the group of students who do not bully and are not bullied. Such changes require a great deal of time and effort, but it is possible, given the necessary support.

The United Nations Charter of Rights for Children states, in part, that:

"Every child has the right to an education and;
Every child has the right to be safe"

N E W Y O R K, March 13 — A third of high school students can think of a classmate who may be troubled enough to stage a violent attack in their school — yet fewer than half have ever had a special class or discussion group that told them how to report a threat of school violence. More than a third also say they've heard a classmate threaten to kill someone — but most of them didn't take it seriously or report it to an adult, according to a new **ABCNEWS/***Good Morning America* poll.

One in eight say they personally know a student who's brought a gun to school, and one in 10 say they've heard of a plan by one or more students at their school to shoot or kill classmates.

At the same time, just a little more than half, 54 percent, says they've had a class, special program or group discussion on the subject of school violence. And just 46 percent have been taught in such a class what to do if they hear a threat or think another student is armed.

On the positive side, the poll found that most students feel safe, and that their concerns are no worse — and in some cases better — than they were after the April 1999 shootings at Columbine High

School in Littleton, Colo. At that time, for instance, 40 percent saw some likelihood of a violent attack at their own school; now it's 29 percent

THE BULLYING FACTOR

Charles Andrew Williams, who is accused of killing two students and wounding, 13 last week in Santee, Calif., reportedly had been a target of bullying at his school. And this poll finds that when students think of a potentially violent classmate, it's generally a boy who comes to mind, and one who's been bullied by others, rather than a bully himself.

Thirty-three percent say they can think of a fellow student "who may be troubled enough to try something like this." That's down a bit from 40 percent in 1999.

Seven in 10 say the potential attacker they can think of is a boy, and 29 percent think of both boys and girls; just 2 percent have only a girl in mind. Three-quarters say it's more likely to be a person who gets picked on than one who picks on others

Poll Results: Attacks & Threats

	3/11/01	4/25/99
Know student who might attack	33%	40%
Heard a student threaten to kill	35%	32%
See some risk of an attack	29%	40%
Know a student who brought a gun to school	13%	20%
Heard a plan to kill students	9%	n/a
Attended a class on school violence	54%	n/a

Had instruction on reporting threats	46%	n/a

Girls are more likely than boys to think their schools should be doing more to deter violence; 41 percent of girls think so, compared to 28 percent of boys. But in other gauges, including personal feelings of safety, there's no real difference between the sexes.

This ABCNEWS poll was conducted by telephone March 8-11 among a random national sample of 500 high school students. The results have a 4.5-point error margin. Fieldwork was done by ICR-International Communications Research of Media, Pa.

Previous ABCNEWS polls can be found on ABCNEWS.com's *Poll Vault*. ■

May 12, 2001 ABC News on the Internet published the following article, which appears to create a summary of the Chapters Ideas.

"A study from the U.S. Secret Service's National Threat Assessment Center found that in about two-thirds of 37 school shootings over the last 25 years, the attackers felt "persecuted, bullied threatened, attacked or injured."

William Pollack, an expert on the psychology of boys, spoke to *Good Morning America*'s Parenting Contributor Ann Pleshette Murphy for the "American Family" series about bullying.

"When we interviewed school shooters, we find that between 50 and 70 percent of them have been viciously bullied and teased," Pollack said. "Now does that mean if you're bullied and teased you're going to pick up a gun? No. But does it mean that those who have gone to the edge are thrown over the edge by being bullied and teased? Absolutely."

The first large-scale national study of bullying by the National Institute of Child Health and Human Development surveyed 15,686

Private and public school pupils in grades 6 through 10. The study found that 10.6 percent of the children had been bullied "sometimes" or "weekly," 13 percent had bullied others, and 6.3 percent had been both the bully and the target of one.

BOYS PUSHED TOWARD TOUGHNESS?

Further, the report found that bullying was more frequent among junior high rather than high school students, and that male students were more likely to be either bullies or the victims of bullies.

Pollack says this is because society pushes boys to be too tough.

"Boys bully because we still bring them up according to what I call the boy code," he said. "That they should be strong and silent, not show their pain and be rough and tough from the age of 2, 3, 4 or 5."

According to a recent survey, 1.6 million children in grades 6 through 10 say they're bullied at least once a week. Fourteen-year-old Doug Smith knows how much that hurts. He's been teased for being short, and teased because his parents are divorced.

"Any kind of teasing, bullying is hard to deal with," Smith said. "But like the stuff where kids like would make fun of my parents being divorced — that you just can't deal with. That's just like getting stabbed in the chest."

And the bullying colored every aspect of his life.

"Every day I would just go crazy," Smith said. "Sometimes it would get to the point where I'd just sit there all alone and just think I really hate him, and it just, it just got really bad. Thank God no one got hurt."

PARENTS DON'T KNOW ABOUT BULLYING

In the sixth grade, when he did not get bullied, his grades were great. But in the seventh grade, when the bullying started, his grades plummeted, Smith said.

"And at some point, you know, kids push too much," said Peter Smith, Doug's father. "And the taunting and the teasing goes on too much."

Both Peter Smith, and his wife, Lorrie Mulhern, knows about the bullying. But researchers say that parents often don't know about their children being bullied. Up to 70 percent of boys maintain a code of silence and never share their pain with their families.

"It's just, you know, it's broken my heart a lot because I know that deep down, my boys want to be those warm, loving, kind, caring people that they're not allowed to be," Mulhern said.

BULLY-BATTLING TACTICS

Most kids who are bullied feel helpless. Pollack has three suggestions, which he shared with Doug Smith.

"One of the things I talk about is that you should recruit other kids to your side," Pollack said. "Create a team of kids who will stop the bully, who will be there with you."

Another idea: talk to a teacher you trust.

"Well I sometimes think if there's one teacher who you know even though they're not in charge of discipline or guidance, but who you feel you can trust, going to them is sometimes really important," Pollack said.

The third tip: Stand up for others.

"Resist the bully's action when he's picking on someone else," Pollack said. "So that when it isn't you, you take the role of saying, hey, actually say stop it."

WHAT CAN PARENTS DO?

May 21 — Some states, including Colorado, are trying to mandate schools to come up with anti-bullying policies.

But some of the education can also begin at home.

Most parents do not know if their children are being bullied at school, but supportive families can make it easier for children who are picked on, *Good Morning America's* Parenting Contributor Ann Pleshette Murphy said.

If your child does not come to you, there are ways to find out if there is a problem. A child who is picked on may seem withdrawn or isolated from family and friends, could exhibit reckless, negative and aggressive behavior, may have lost regular friends, or show signs of depression. It is hard to get boys to talk, so parents might try using action-talk to get boys to open up, Murphy says.

Parents should not call the bully's parents.

"The worst thing parents can do is try to contact the bully's parents," Murphy says. "You have to allow the child to be involved in the situation."

And although a parent's first instinct may be to tell the child to fight back, there are other alternatives.

Parents should, however, find out if a bully is dangerous or lethal, get school administration involved, and gather a group of parents to complain."

No matter how hard we try the school will have to continue to work on controlling the problem of the school bully. It may be a beneficial place to start if each school has in place a program where students have the opportunity to look at the issue of the school bully, what happens to there peers if it goes unchecked and the possible consequences that could arise not only for the individual but also for the school and community at large. Enough has been written and has been on the local and national news programs that students can easily build a base of information from which to work in understanding and reducing, if not eliminating the problem. (See Chapter Ten for Activity involving this Chapters Content)

SUMMARY

No matter how hard we try the school will have to continue to work on controlling the problem of the school bully. It may be a beneficial place to start if each school has in place a program where students have the opportunity to look at the issue of the school bully, what happens to there peers if it goes unchecked and the possible consequences that could arise not only for the individual but also for the school and community at large. Enough has been written and has been on the local and national news programs that students can easily build a base of information from which to work in understanding and reducing, if not eliminating the problem. See Chapter Ten

CHAPTER FIVE

PROMOTING GOOD BEHAVIOR DISCIPLINE TECHNIQUES

After the teacher has laid out their goals and objectives and has completed the planning stages for the classroom it should become an environment for promoting good behavior on a daily bases. This chapter is devoted to the process of promoting good discipline in the classroom and a look at various discipline techniques that might be helpful in achieving the goals and objectives hoped for in the classroom. The authors of this text would like to emphasis a positive discipline approach for the classroom and will work in defining this approach through the use of various recommendations and techniques throughout the chapter.

Although there is no magic process to obtaining effective classroom discipline there are certain elements that can and will lead to effective discipline. Some of these elements are effective communications skills; developing a planned strategy, setting an example for students by being aware of the role model each educator plays in the process, learning to develop positive attitude that will "rub off" on the student, motivation, reducing conflict, setting guidelines, and using various techniques that will allow the student the ability to respond in a positive and effective manner while knowing that they have ownership in the process.

There have been many discipline plans devised over the years, each with positive elements that can be used in the classroom. Some educators have used assertive Discipline very effectively. Others have used positive Discipline, reducing the emphasis on rules. There is a wide range of plans, and combination of techniques, all which are good when they are effective in the classroom. Each often depends greatly on the uniqueness of the student population as well as the individual instructor.

Just as in curriculum design and implementation, the teacher must assume the responsibility for playing the important, ongoing role in behavior development. This means that he/she must become involved as a designer and facilitator of behavior motivation, student actions and activities. Teachers must be concerned with the fact that, in the long run, student behavior is a direct result of instructional actions, curriculum demands, school policy, and performance success on the part of the student as an individual and the class as a whole.

THE TEACHER AS A ROLE MODEL

Students learn from their environment and imitate what they see. We are aware of this from what each student brings from their own individual family and cultural environment in the way they act, react, and the language they use. It is therefore essential that as educators we provide a positive role model for the students in the school environment. If we as teachers want to drink coffee, eat in the classroom, or spend time visiting with other co-workers students will wish to do the same.

There are a number of traits and practices that each teacher can review and do a self-evaluation as it relates to them as a role model for students. (See appendix). The traits and practices may come naturally for some, and for others they provide an opportunity to improve.

1. **Educators need to walk with dignity.** Students can imitate the teacher who does not slouch, walk with their hands in their pockets, and chew gum or toothpicks.

2. **Gestures.** The teacher must show no Weakness, and avoids affectation, being overly graceful, keeping gestures simple, strong and Infrequent.

3. **Use of voice.** When speaking keep your head up, face forward, projecting your voice, so all can hear. The message must sound important to the student

4. **The use of speech.** Do the things you say sound sincere and convinced, accurate and informed or does the student pay little attention due to lack of your delivery?

5. **Temperament-Disposition.** Are you cheerful and self-confident, remaining even tempered.

6. **Acceptance.** Do you feel accepted by the Students, co-workers? Do you show this to the students?

7. **Scholarly.** The successful teacher in the classroom is knowledgeable of the subject matter and provides the class with his/her clear convictions of the subject matter? If a question arises regarding the subject matter, are you willing to admit error or be willing to share your need to research the subject matter? Students will react favorably to you and will share this same trait in their own learning process.

8. **Teaching the subject.** As a role model for the student are you willing to listen to the student's ideas in planning the learning process? Are you willing to try various types of activities to teach facts and skills such as explanation, illustration, memorization, questioning, problem-solving, library research and laboratory approaches?

9. **School Awareness.** The educator should be aware of the schools policies and procedures, schedule and calendar and support the policies of the school. This does not imply that you cannot disagree with them, however it is inappropriate to disagree with the policies and procedures with the students.

10. **Maturity.** Are you fulfilling the duty to be the kind of person you want your students to be? It is necessary to be proud of your profession, show mental sharpness, have a wide range of interests and be professional in your outlook, philosophy and objectives in life. When disagreements arise, is a mature approach used toward these differences and misunderstandings with a willingness to learn and compromise when necessary?

11. **Communication.** As role models we provide students with an appropriate method of communication by retaining eye contact, keeping an open mind throughout the conversation, hold to the subject of the conversation, ask for clarification of areas that we do not understand, visibly respond with appropriatefacial and body gestures and think about what is being said rather than how we plan to respond.

12. **Caring** although listed last, this element is no doubt one of the most important when dealing with students on a day to day basis. Students, no matter what age level or level of intelligence can tell when the teacher cares about them and who they are as individuals and as part of the total classroom.

The teacher, as a role model, can enhance the discipline process in a very positive way simply by providing for the students an example of what they wish the student to be. Students will imitate the teacher as they do most adults they are in contact with throughout their day.

PLANNED DISCIPLINE STRATEGIES

How common it is to hear advice from co-workers such as "Don't Smile Until Christmas ". If you smile and appear happy or friendly your students will take advantage of you. If you force strict discipline on the students the first few months you will whip the students into shape." This philosophy however may create more problems for you than it will alleviate. It certainly is not helpful in creating an appropriate learning environment. This is the time when you're developing of goals and objectives as well as your classroom organization will pay huge dividends for you. Planning the strategy will promote good behavior. Steps you will want to consider are:

1. Identify the problem.
2. Develop theories about the causes and how the problem may be solved.
3. Test your theories by observation. Design an intervention program that you can try, evaluate and revise if necessary.
4. Enlist the aid of other individuals who come in contact with the student(s).
5. Correct the behavior problems as soon as possible. If the problem is allowed to continue for any length of time it is much more difficult to correct.
6. Balance the corrective measures with positive feedback.
7. Use a variety of techniques to have the student make the transition from the negative activity to a positive activity. Not all techniques work well when repeated time and again.
8. Arouse interest in positive behavior by relating what he students have achieved in the past with a current situation.
9. It is sometimes necessary to use structured learning.
10. Provide clear instructions making sure the student is fully aware of your expectations.
11. Try "bonding" with the students if possible by spending the needed time with them outside of the classroom environment. (At recess, before or after school, during lunch or extra curricular activities.)

The amount of time you give to developing these strategies will pay off many fold in establishing good behavior and will save both instructional and personal time in the future.

MOTIVATION OF STUDENTS

The best type of discipline is self - discipline; so to is it true that the best type of motivation is self - motivation. However, we are aware that in the classroom setting, not all students are self-disciplined or self - motivated.

In order to have good discipline the educator must work and develop a motivational plan for the classroom. How this plan will finally look will depend on the age and grade level of the student as well as the social and cultural experience the student has experienced. The teachers own attitude has much to do with students adopting or not adopting effective motives, just as the teacher's attitude is responsible for how little the student accomplishes. To achieve motivation with students a number of elements might be considered by the educator when dealing with students. The educator should ask themselves a number of questions:

1. Am I friendly to the students I come in contact with?
2. Am I understanding and tolerant of the student?
3. Do I like the students at the grade, age level that I am working?.
4. Am I firm, but fair with the students?
5. Do I recognize the efforts of the group or individual student and reward those efforts?
6. Do I maintain discipline and classroom control, so that all students have an equal opportunity to learn - remembering that students need a quiet, organized environment?
7. Do I know my subject, and how to teach it, how to make it interesting and be enthusiastic? about it?
8. Am I teaching about areas the students are interested in that are included in the curriculum?

Try to start where your class is; by fitting the assignments, tests, class work, and type of learning to the student. Teach your class study methods for their specific grade and age level. Students need to learn how to read an assignment. Assignments should be tailored in such a way that it allows for individual differences in student ability. Requiring the same assignment for all students allows for failure on the part of the slower student and boredom on the part of the more academically inclined student. Resources should be provided for the different type of learner whenever possible.

How often have we experienced waiting days or even weeks for assignments or a take home test to be returned? When the teacher plans their time well and provides immediate feedback to the student the student will feel what they have completed is important and the self- motivation level increases. We all want to know where we stand; this is evidenced in our family and social life. The educational setting is no different.

It is critical in the motivational and discipline process that the teacher knows their students. Some techniques to use in getting to know your students are:

1. Page through school yearbooks, newspapers and programs to get to know the likes and dislikes of the student. This information placed on a 3 x 5 index card can be used over and over again throughout the year.
2. Individual scores. The information is excellent to compare homework and test results with the student's ability to complete the assignments.
3. An interesting technique that has been used is the classroom is to have the student write an autobiography the first day of school. The information contained in the autobiography is useful in determining the language skills, interests and areas of insecurity on the part of the student. If the student is aware that the autobiography is not going to be shared with their peers they are often more open and direct - which of course is the hope of the teacher.
4. Establish rapport with the student and class as soon as possible. Greet the class cheerfully when you meet them each

day. Let each day be a NEW day and an opportunity for a new beginning.

POSITIVE REINFORCEMENT

Positive reinforcement is one of the most basic tools for creating and maintaining classroom discipline. Reinforcement can be anything, which encourages the repetition of desired behavior. In order for the reinforcement to be positive, the reinforcement must be of value to the student. We as educators often forget that what is of value to us may not be of value to an individual student. What is of value to one student however, may not be of value to another. Thus, a teacher might wish to have a variety of positive statements and rewards to meet the needs of a diverse classroom. The unique requirement of positive reinforcement is the teacher must "catch" the student being good. This process has a variety of positive impacts on the classroom.

There are three basic types of positive rewards. The first is the tangible reward. It may include tokens, stars on a chart, certificates, stickers or free reading time. The second is a social reward, which includes, praise, compliments, attention and other types of verbal and non-verbal feedback. Using positive enabling statements such as: You have done an excellent job on that assignment even though there were a few errors that you will need to address, your work is improving a little each day, will in essence motivate the student. Not all students require the same level of positive reinforcement but each student should receive it on a regular basis. The third type of positive reinforcement is self-reinforcement, which occurs when the child feels or experiences a sense of achievement or self-satisfaction.

Teachers must be careful to remain aware of how they are giving positive reinforcement. Giving to much or to little is not effective, however finding the balance for each student can be extremely rewarding to the process. The educator needs to be sure that positive reinforcement is applied to a desired behavior.

"Nothing succeeds like success". When motivating students towards good discipline through positive reinforcement, success will occur for the teacher, but more importantly for the student with the ultimate goal being self - motivation for success and appropriate discipline within the classroom setting.

THE IMPORTANCE OF SELF-ESTEEM IN DISCIPLINE

When an educator strives to promote good discipline in the classroom it is crucial that some quality time is spent on developing self - esteem among the students. When we survey the students we find that most often students who lack self-esteem are the same students who are discipline problems. Keeping this in mind it is therefore beneficial to promote self-esteem as part of the total discipline program.

Students with low self-esteem tend to be more troubled by depression, anxiety, irritability and aggression. Another result of low self-esteem in students is shyness and social awkwardness, which can lead to a need for acceptance by others. In turn this need for acceptance often leads to discipline problems in the classroom and the total school environment.

The foundations for low or high self-esteem seem to surface early in a child's life. Most kindergarten and first grade teachers can point out the student who has a problem with self-esteem. If this is so, then it is critical that the educator develop positive self-esteem strategies in the early grades and that teachers continue to work toward positive self-esteem throughout the educational process at all grade levels. In today's society we see children joining gangs, committing suicide, involved in serious crimes and being major problems to the educational setting. The authors believe that along with good planning and organization, the incorporation of exercises to develop self-esteem will resolve many of these problems in the classroom.

In a study (Stanley Coppersmith, 1967, 1975) it was found that boys had a higher level of self-esteem when the following occurred. Parents Showed more affection, Showed interest in children's activities, Were more accepting of their children, Used sound and consistent discipline, and Had a high level of self-esteem themselves.

The study can be helpful to educators in two ways. The first item of the five items listed above when working with parents could be used as a point of discussion to elevate the child's self-esteem and secondly, educators can readily place the five points into place on a daily basis when working with children to raise self-esteem.

It is common for all individuals to judge themselves in how they succeed and compare themselves to others. Students do this on a daily basis in the area of academics, sports and all other ares of competition. As educators we will need to address and work with students helping them develop realistic goals for themselves and avoid developing low self-esteem.

Students tend to compare themselves with others in their own unique educational setting, rather than looking at a hypothetical setting. They should be guided in the area of public presentation that is, presenting themselves to others in social interactions.

We know too, that students look at us, as educators, as models. We therefore must model self-esteem for them. Children look at their own race group for example and role models. This includes ethic groups as well as sex. As educators then, we can and should provide within the curriculum opportunities for the students to have the opportunity to meet and interact with individuals that can be role models for them.

Some basic guidelines to consider when working with children are as follows in the development of positive self-esteem:

1. Students need to recognize that they alone control their self-esteem. Recognizing this fact students need to be taught to dwell on the positive feedback they receive from others rather than the negative feedback. Students with low self-esteem generally dwell on the negative feedback they receive. We as educators when giving corrective statements should be aware of the negative feedback we share with students and strive to make our corrections and directives in a positive manner.
2. Encourage the students to set their own goals rather than letting others set them. Many people, including our own selves have gone through life in a career that is not of our own

choosing but rather one that was set for us by the coaxing of a parent or teacher. Often when individuals are in this type of setting they never obtain real success and feel they are failures. One tends to be happier and has a higher level of achievement by setting and having ownership of our life goals.

When working with students, educators should teach the student to evaluate and make decisions for themselves. This does not exclude listening to others, but it does place the final decision on the individual student.

3. Students need to be realistic in setting their goals. If they are not realistic, they build on failure. Even when the student truly values certain goals and ideals, they may not always be realistic. Certain limitations occur for all of us when setting goals for ourselves. Finances, certain handicaps and academic abilities all play a critical role in the goal setting process.

   As educators, when working with students we should, in a positive manner, point out to the student what may be realistic for them, keeping in mind that the final decision again remains with them.

4. Students need to modify negative thinking and self talk. When something positive happens many individuals attribute it to good luck. If something negative happens they tend to take the blame. This in turn creates negative self-esteem.

   The educator, when working with students, needs to point out that in life itself, both the positive and negative occurs for all of us. We should dwell on the positive and set aside the negative experiences we face on an on going basis.

5. Students need to emphasize their strengths. Individuals who have low self-esteem often derive little satisfaction from their successes. Each individual has strengths and weaknesses. It is important to develop and nurture the points within us that are positive and are considered strengths. We need to let go of the weakness and build on the strengths we each process. Students who work to improve themselves by focusing on the

positive will succeed. Working to improve one also requires that the student reassess goals on a regular bases.
6. Approaching others with a positive attitude will improve the entire outlook one has for oneself as well as a person's outlook toward other individuals. The outcome of this process will be a positive feeling within themselves as well as those whom they interact with on a daily bases.

If we as educators can instill this concept in students many of the discipline problems we face each day will fade quickly and permanently in the educational setting.

GETTING ALONG / CONFLICT RESOLUTION

In the development of good classroom discipline an essential element that the teacher must consider is his/her skills in the area of conflict resolution. Entire workshops, texts and courses are available to help the educator in this area. It is suggested that all educators avail themselves of one of the above opportunities whenever possible.

Many discipline problems can be resolved by using simple techniques of conflict resolution. Before applying these basic guidelines the educator must first consider the level of maturity of the student and design the application to the child. A few simple guidelines are as follows:

1. Withdraw from the power struggle to allow for a cooling-off period.
2. Handle the problem on one-to-one bases. Try not to involve individuals that are not part of the conflict.
3. Remember that a conflict is not one sided. Youboth have the problem. Try to enter the resolution, with the idea that you are not enemies.
4. Remember that everyone involved has feelings. A conflict cannot be resolved when you are not aware of the other persons feelings are not sensitive to their hurt and fear.

5. Everyone has his or her own agenda. The student is no different than the teacher. The teacher as well as the student should be aware of the various reasons each individual has in the conflict and understands them completely.
6. Everyone has his or her own point of view. No one is 100 per cent correct therefore there is room for discussion and the give and take process.
7. Remember there are many ways to resolve a problem. Be willing to look at the various options that may be available.
8. Look at the options available and make sure that all parties are happy with the final agreement and that the agreement is sound and workable within the educational or classroom setting. Do not agree to something that will not meet with the requirements of the school, parents or co - workers if they are to be involved.

PUNISHMENTS / ALTERNATIVES

Punishment can be any type of unpleasant stimulus to discourage a specific unfavorable behavior. Punishment is a **negative** form of discipline and should only be used selectively and only in conjunction with a positive form of discipline. There are three basic forms of punishment; physical, verbal and ignoring. The authors do not subscribe to any of the above. Although punishment can provide an immediate feedback its long lasting effect is extremely limited. Too often punishment will bring about additional discipline problems for the teacher in the classroom. This is not to say that consequences should not occur for behavior that is undesirable on the part of the student. A positive consequence can be both a learning experience for the child as well as effective in the elimination of the discipline problem. Such consequences may be parental contact, detention (where the child has time to spend with the teacher to work on resolving the problem), or a learning activity that will enhance the academic skills of the student. Students in each case should fully understand why the consequence was given and the expected outcomes. When the teacher deals with alternatives to "punishment" as defined above, he/she is helping the student find individual ways in succeeding and contributing to acceptable behavior patterns.

Alternatives to punishment are not always easy to implement. They require the teacher to be perceptive, resourceful, organized, consistent, enthusiastic and supportive to all students. Alternatives require extra work, however the rewards will pay off for the teacher in effective classroom discipline.

TECHNIQUES TO CONSIDER

Techniques that work for one teacher or grade level may not work for another teacher or grade level. The following ideas are provided as a "seed " for the teacher and it is suggested that the teacher develop specific techniques for their grade level or subject area. (See appendix) The teacher has a certain amount of latitude in the classroom, however it is prudent to make sure that the specific technique meets the philosophy of the school prior to implementing it with the students.

1. **Use of voice.** - Three levels of voice may be implemented. Begin with a soft voice for first and second commands, building to a more aggressive voice for repeated reprimands. As a last resort the teacher's voice might show strong anger but not increase in volume.

2. **Begin the class** each day with a start up actively. An example would be a mathematics problem or an English sentence on the board that is to be completed within the first few minutes of the class period. This allows the teacher to have the time to answer questions of individual students, take attendance and do other administrative requirements. Students have an immediate learning activity, thus reducing the need for direction. Students are placed on task.

3. **A time** - out corner can be very helpful for the student who has difficulty with a behavioral expectation. It provides time - out for the Student as well as lessons the need for an immediate reaction from the teacher giving the teacher and student a cooling-off period.

4. **A response - cost system.** This technique provides an automatic "cost" either a written assignment, or extra duty, for a response that is unacceptable according to the goals and objectives established for the classroom. Care needs to be given that the assignment does not discourage the student from enjoying tithe subject matter at a liking the activity at a later datm or on school grounds and is given at the discretion of the teacher. The certificate may result in extra library time, increased rest room privileges, free reading time or any other reward, which fits the individual classroom. The certificates should not be "tied" to grades for accomplished academic work.

5. **A Chart** - Keep a chart for attendance. This may `encourage student to obtain proper attendance or being in the right place at the right time.

6. **A sign** - out book for the use of the rest room. Each student (based on school policy) may leave for the rest room during class time a set or limited number of times per quarter. This is an effective procedure, which eliminates a great deal of hassle in the classroom.

7. **The use of tokens, chips, stamps,** savings book or bogus money can be a positive reinforcement for work completed, based upon the guidelines developed in the classroom.

8. **Regular behavior reports** sent to parents indicating the student's behavior in the classroom. This can be used at any level, however the reports should be written so that the statements are of a

positive nature. Reports should be sent for both positive and negative behavior.

9. **Parent conferences** - The idea that a conference with a parent should only be held when the school schedules them is limiting and restricting to the discipline process Teachers should feel free to meet with a parent at anytime throughout the year and students should be aware of the teacher's policy regarding these conferences.

10. **Thank you notes** - Thank you notes to the student as well as the parent is a positive approach, which will reinforce good discipline within the classroom. These notes, when sent through the mail, are even more effective. Mailing reduces peer pressure and allows the student the opportunity to make the decision of which they wish to share the information.

11. **Inquiry notes** - A note of inquiry regarding a student sent to the school counselor or special area teacher requesting information (using positive statements)about a student can result in benefits both from other staff members as well as being a positive reinforcement for the student.

12. **Award programs** - Most schools have an award program for the school either on a semester or yearly bases. These programs provide incentives for the student. An award program on a quarterly or grading period bases in the classroom can be beneficial in motivating the student in the academic areas as well as the area of self - discipline.

13. **Talk time** - An interesting concept that students enjoy is an assigned talk time, generally at the end of the class period, for earned good behavior. It reduces the need for discipline in the classroom and provides the students an opportunity for sharing with fellow classmates.

14. **Comic Books/Magazines** - Obtaining good comic books/magazines and having them available that are appropriate to the student's grade level and maturity can be a reward that is easily controlled within the classroom.

15. **Duties** - Many students find that being assigned a duty can be a very rewarding experience. It provides the student with responsibility and recognition that they may otherwise not receive.

16. **Contracting** - The concept of contracting with a student w5ho is a discipline problem can be very effective in increasing positive self-discipline. In contracting the agreement may be either between the student and teacher or may include school co-workers and / or parents. Contracts place the responsibility for behavior on the student. Contracts when written must be reasonable and agreed upon by all parties involved. The use of the conflict-resolution process works well in developing contracts with students.

17. **Student Conferences** - Holding conferences with students (away from the normal classroom time) is an effective instrument in working with discipline problems. It is an excellent opportunity for the student and teacher to share and listen to each other.

18. **Log Keeping** - This approach can be effective as it requires the student to keep a log or record of each time they have been corrected for an unacceptable behavior or infraction of the guidelines that have been established in the Organization/managements portion of the discipline plan. Record keeping can be used for discipline problems, incomplete homework or other infractions. A certain cause – effect relationship should be developed with the student based on the number of entries in their log.

19. **Asking Questions** - When asking questions, never use the name of the student before asking the question. This hopefully, will give you the attention of the whole class. (See appendix) Classroom Questions - What Kind

20. **Ability**- Call on both boys and girls with high and low ability equally. Students are quick to size up the teacher if a pattern is set where the teacher generally calls on a student they feel know the answer.

21. **Quizzes** - Have a thought provoking quiz ready if the class does not wish to cooperate. Use this technique rarely. It can be extremely effective if the teacher needs time to regroup and plan an effective strategy.

22. **Whole Class Discipline** - This technique can be effective as it allows all students to become involved in the discipline process. It can provide students an opportunity to discuss their ideas and concerns with the teacher. If the entire class receives a consequence they should be aware of the reason for the entire class receiving the consequence and what alternatives might be available in the future.

23. **Extinction** - Extinction is the concept that negative behaviors can be eliminated by the withdrawal of reinforcement. Since attention is basically a reinforcement process and many students are discipline problems due to the need for attention the extinction process can be effective on a limited basis. The teacher when using this process needs to be assured that peer attention is also withdrawn, or the process will be ineffective. Talking to the other students and gaining their support, prior to using this process is essential.

24. **Face the students** - It is important when starting out the class that the teacher faces the students when they enter the room. If you have hall or supervisory duty stand in the doorway and let the students know that you can see them. Be visible.

25. **Seating students** - Students have a tendency to walk about the room when entering. As part of your class rules your expectations

should have been defined to the students. Do not yell at them or verbalize the direction, simply wave down the direction with a gesture of your hand. Students will soon realize what is expected.

26. **Administrative duties** - Complete as much of the daily administrative duties as possible, either before the students arrive or at the end of the previous day. This allows you time to view the class and control students, thus reducing confusion and discipline problems.

27. **Speaking voice** - Speak more loudly, clearly and slowly at the beginning of the period. Speak to the student in the back of the room and at a normal conversation rate. What you say at the beginning of a class is generally more important than later in the class period.

28. **Chalkboard** – When using the chalkboard write tall, <u>heavy and clearly</u>. Not all students have the same vision. This will eliminate students having to talk to others seeking information on what has been written. The use of an easel or overhead projector can be useful in maintaining good discipline as it allow the teacher to face the class at all times and the material can be prepared ahead of the actual class presentation. The materials can be saved for review and reattaching through the use of these mediums.

29. **Move about** - In maintaining good discipline it is Essential that the teacher move about the classroom. This is more important during the first part of the lesson, as it provides the teacher an opportunity to check to see that all students are on task.

MODELS FOR GUIDING CLASSROOM DISCIPLINE

Along with specific techniques, it should be mentioned that a number of well-known educators have developed key ideas for classroom discipline. We would be remiss in writing a book regarding discipline to ignore the ideas of others. Although the ideas may be different than ours, teachers should consider them as valid and borrow from those elements that may be useful to their individual classroom needs and environment.

The following models for are key ideas from six different authors. (Source: Building Classroom Discipline: From Models to Practice. C.M.Charles.1985)

1. **Skinners Key Ideas.** Behavior modification.

    Behavior is shaped by its consequences

    <u>Behavior</u> is strengthened if followed by reinforces

    <u>Behavior</u> is weakened if not followed by

    Reinforcement-<u>Strengthened</u> behaviors are most

    likely to be repeated.<u>Behavior</u> is weakened if

    followed by punishment. - <u>Systematic</u> use of

    reinforcement can shape individual behavior

    - In the early state of learning, constant reinforcement produces the best results

    - Once learned and at desired level, reinforcement maintained through intermittent

    - When applied to classroom learning and discipline, process of behavior shaping through reinforcement is called behavior modification

- Behavior modification is one of the most powerful tools to educators

- Behavior modification successfully uses various kinds of reinforces

2. **Ginott's Key Ideas**

   - Discipline is a series of little victories

   - The most important ingredient in discipline is the teacher's own self-discipline.

   - The second most important is in using same massages when correcting students

   - Teachers at their best use congruent communication that is harmonious with students own feelings

   - Teachers at their worst attack and label student characters

   - Teachers should model the behavior they hope to see

   - Inviting cooperation from students is preferable to demanding it

   - Teachers should express anger but inappropriate sane ways

   - Labeling students disables them

   - Sarcasm and praise often are dangerous; use both with great care

   - Apologies from students should be accepted with the understanding that they intend to improve

= The best teachers help students to build their own self-esteem and to trust their own experience

3. **Gasser's Key Ideas.**

    - Students are rational beings; they can control their behavior

    - Good choices produce good behavior; bad choices produce bad behavior

    - Teachers must forever try to help students make good choices

    - Teachers who truly care about their students accept no excuses for bad behavior

    - Reasonable consequences should always follow student behavior, good or bad

    - Class rules are essential and they must be enforced.

    - Classroom meetings are effective vehicles for attending to matters of class rules, behavior and discipline

4. **Dreikurs Key Ideas**

    - Discipline is not punishment. It is teaching students to impose limits on themselves

    - Democratic teachers provide firm guidance and leadership; they allow student to have a say in establishing rules and consequences

    - All students want to belong; they want status and recognition, all of their behaviors indicate efforts to belong

- Misbehavior reflects the mistaken belief that it will gain students the recognition they want

- Misbehavior is associated with four mistaken goals: attention getting, power seeking, revenge and displaying inadequacy

- Teachers should identify mistaken goals and then act in ways that do not reinforce them

- Teachers should strive to encourage student's efforts, but avoid praising their work or character

- Teachers should teach students that

    Unpleasant consequences would always follow their inappropriate behavior

5. **Jones' Key Ideas**

    - Teachers in typical classrooms lose approximately fifty percent of their instructional time because students are off task or disturbing the teacher or class

    - Practically all this lost time results in two kinds of student misbehavior thinking

    - Without permission and general goofing off including making noises, daydreaming, or getting out ones' seats without asking permission

    - Most of this lost teaching time can be salvaged if teachers systematically employ three kinds of techniques that strongly assist discipline:
        1) Effective body language
        2) Incentive systems

3) Efficient individual help good classroom discipline results mainly from the first...effective body language, which includes posture, eye contact, facial expressions, signals, gestures, and physical proximity
- Incentive systems motivate students to remain on task, to complete work and to behave properly ... also contribute strongly to good discipline

6. **Canter Key Ideas**

   - Teachers should insist on decent, responsible behavior from their students

   - Teacher failure for all practical purposes, is synonymous with student failure

   - Many teachers labor under false assumptions about discipline, they believe that firm control is stifling and inhumane; it is not, firm control maintained correctly in humane and liberating

   - Teachers have basic educational rights in their classroom; they have the right to establish optional learning environments and the right to determine, request and expect appropriate behavior from students and the right to receive help from administrators and parents

   - Students have basic rights in the classroom, they have the right to have teachers help them limit their inappropriate self destructive behavior... the right to have teachers provide positive support and the right to chose how to behave

   - Needs, rights and conditions are best met through assertive discipline

ASSERTIVE DISCIPLINE CONSISTS OF THE FOLLOWING ELEMENTS

1) Identifying expectations clearly
2) Willingness to say, "I like this and I don't like that"
3) Persistence in stating expectations and feelings
4) Use of firm tone of voice
5) Maintenance of eye contact
6) Use of nonverbal gestures in support
7) Assertive discipline

SUMMARY

In summary promoting good discipline and using effective discipline techniques is an ongoing process in the classroom. There are no specific techniques or quick fix answers for the educational profession as a whole. There are certain ideas that can be applied and modified for individual teachers and classroom settings. Promoting good behavior is essential for the learning process to be effectively accomplished. This process helps not only the student but also just as important makes teaching enjoyable and reduces burn out on the part of the educator.

CHAPTER SIX

ADMINISTRATION CO - WORKERS

Although the ultimate responsibility for effective classroom discipline lies with the individual teacher there are times that the teacher will want other school personnel involved in the process. Classroom discipline that can be adequately handled by the teacher is the most effective and a longer lasting form of discipline.

The school administration, principal, assistant principal or dean is in a position to have a tremendous impact on student behavior. The effectiveness of the administration however, depends largely on the skill of the teacher who implements the administrator's policies. Working closely with the school administration and co-workers is essential in maintaining good discipline. There must exist, in this process cooperation and full understanding of the role each member of the administration and staff play in the discipline process. The discipline process can work very effectively for the teacher when there is an understanding of and respect for each individual's role.

Administrators are not teachers, and likewise, teachers are not administrators. The administrative role is to provide support and in-service and to create policies to guide teachers in the implementation of the school rules and procedures regarding these policies. Hopefully, these policies and rules will be developed with the teaching staff in a collaborative manner. Administrative members of the school environment should regularly visit the classroom so that they can not only be aware of the classroom environment, but show support for the teacher's classroom objectives and management plan for discipline.

Any discipline plan designed by the teacher should be shared with the administration and the support of the administration should be solicited. If other co-workers are involved, the same communication is essential for good discipline. It takes only one administrator or co-worker to "upset the apple cart" by undermining the discipline plan of a specific teacher.

The teacher must know how to elicit the cooperation of administration and co-workers in the discipline process. One very important way of doing this is to share your discipline objectives, plan, and maintenance process with those you work. In the sharing of the information the teacher should clearly spell out what their expectations of administration and co - workers are. By doing so it allows for the lines of communication to remain open, especially during times of crisis, when the teacher feels he cannot handle a discipline problem on his own.

QUESTIONS TO ASK

The teacher should ask a few simple questions when dealing with administration and co-workers. Typical questions might be:

1. Do I maintain my position of responsibility and leadership, through friendly helpful actions and attitudes?
2. Do I encourage a sense of teamwork among the faculty?
3. Do I give the administration and co - workers a sense of backing them in their ideas and decisions?
4. Do I work to establish common school wide goalsrelating to the discipline process?
5. Do I give administration and co -workers the feeling that I am anxious to understand their problems as well a expecting them to understand mine?
6. Am I consistent and just in my requests when dealing with problem students?

7. Do I avoid the use of threats and ultimatums that may be impossible to carry out by the administration and co - workers?
8. Do I constantly seek to develop a "team" sense in dealing with discipline problems?
9. Do I know how to laugh at myself?
10. Am I comfortable with sharing my discipline and management guidelines with my co - workers?
11. Am I open to suggestions and willing to try new ideas?

SEEKING HELP

Teachers should be comfortable in the knowledge that when they seek help that they will receive help in the discipline process. It is also important that everyone on the faculty understands that seeking help to solve discipline problems does not imply personal weakness on the part of the educator. It is just as much a crime to allow a class to be disrupted by a few as it is to hide the fact that a problem with discipline exists. The more expedient a problem can be identified, which may take the help of a school psychologist, counselor or specially trained staff member, the sooner the problem can be cured.

Recent court, school board or central office decisions often place the administrators in charge of discipline in the school in a position that they may not be able to support the teacher in a way the teacher may wish. Teachers must understand that in many cases a child may not be suspended for an infraction. Alternative methods of discipline must seriously be considered.

The teacher has the responsibility to work with his/her fellow staff a member in preparing in advance alternative consequences for infractions of school polices. Along with this concept, the teacher should make the administration aware of potential student problems so that they may be addressed early on in the year.

COOPERATING WITH OTHERS

Working with administration and co-workers at times is not an easy task. However, all members of a school faculty generally have a common goal and want effective discipline in both their individual educational setting as well as the school as a whole. The following suggestions can be helpful in achieving the desired end result:

- Make an appointment to talk about and share your discipline problems with administration and co - workers.
- Take a leadership role in working with other faculty members on discipline techniques.
- Be willing to serve on committees that will address your needs and the needs of the school.
- Assume leadership in working with other school personnel; such as counselors, psychologists, special education teachers and administration.
- Develop the ability to work as a team.
- Develop your ability to share responsibility for good discipline or the lack thereof.
- Develop the ability to share or join your own discipline techniques with those of others.
- Develop the ability to collaborate with others.
- Develop the ability to be help and be helped.
- Be willing to supervise, be supervised and critique discipline procedures.

SUMMARY

The best advice is to use administration and co-workers as resource personal, dealing with each individual with an open mind and a positive attitude. Involve the faculty in both the positive and negative elements of the discipline process, remembering that the most effective classroom discipline is that which is fair, organized and consistent.

Chapter SEVEN

PARENTS

Some years ago a principal made a statement suggesting two specific ideas to his teaching staff as they relate to school discipline and the role of parents. These ideas have surfaced throughout the years. It is important for both classroom teachers' and school administrators/ to be cognizant of these ideas when addressing discipline and parents.

The first concept is that parents are the **PRIME EDUCATORS** of their children and teachers must fully understand and buy into this fact. As educators we can do a great deal in forming students attitudes and providing them with the necessary skills and life goals. However true this may be, we are either limited or enriched by the background that the student brings with them to the educational setting. Assuming that the parent is the "prime educator "of their child we must do everything within our power to enhance this concept and include the parent in the total educational process. In doing so we increase our ability to achieve the goals we have set forth for the students. This basic concept provides us a working relationship and the necessary support of the parent/guardian. This support is critical, especially in the discipline process.

The second concept stated was there is no formal course or educational program that parents receive prior to the beginning of the raising of his or her children. We as educators have a responsibility not to tell parents how to raise their children, but rather to provide them with goals, concepts, and assistance in dealing with the child at a given age. This philosophy will help the professional educator to "turn on "parents to the formal educational mechanism and allow for a cooperative effort to occur between the educator and the parent. Parents, just as educators, are turned off when they do not have ownership to the process we are involved in. Parents are protective of their children, but can also be open minded and cooperative if we instill in them the feeling of need and understanding.

FAMILIES DIFFER

When working with parents, we as educators must also realize that families (parents) differ from each other for many reasons.

1. Families due, to cultural heritage experiences, have different ways of showing affection. Some parents are more demonstrative than others. The quiet reserved parent is likely to give the impression that they do not love as much as the more demonstrative one. Then too, parents who have had am unhappy childhood experience or have been in a marriage that was not pleasant often make up for this by lavishing affection on their children. The teacher needs to be aware, as much as possible, of these situations when dealing with the student.
2. Different parents set dissimilar standards for a child's behavior. What a parent expects from a child depends largely on what was expected of them when they were children. For example, if a father was expected as a child to earn money to help the family, he may expect the same from his children. It can be a different case when the parent's childhood was so strict that it brought about resentments in their life. When that child becomes a parent he /she may go to the opposite end of the spectrum and allow the child unlimited freedoms.
3. Parents have different expectations of their children depending upon their own success or failure in life. A parent who has been either a high or low achiever has a tendency to expect

respectfully more or less from their children who is an average achiever.

4. Families also differ in their social and economic standing within the community where they live. A child whose parents can give him "everything" tends to become a disturbing influence in a group of students who parents cannot give them as much materially. Some students have a strong resentment toward others who are not within their social or economic class, which emerges within the classroom and can cause further discipline problems.

5. Differences in family size play a significant role in the discipline process as well. The child from the large family has advantages and disadvantages just as the child from the small family. The teacher should become aware of the size of the family as well as the ages of siblings within the family structure. The order of birth of the child in the family should also be considered as older siblings are generally given different freedoms and responsibilities than younger ones.

PARENT COMMUNICATION

Students can be motivated towards good discipline if we as educators use the home to provide a portion of this motivation. There are a number of ways in which we incorporate this concept to the classroom setting:

1. Keep the parents up-to-date on their child's success and failure. We often communicate with parents only when there is a negative situation occurring in the classroom or school. Negativism enhances negativism. All parents need to hear about the positive actions of their child as well as those areas needing improvement.

2. Point out and ask questions about how they can help their child overcome certain weaknesses. Parents, in most cases know their child better than the classroom teacher.

3. Work to acquire the parents' cooperation and their help in controlling the student's actions. They may provide a support level at home that will compliment the goals and procedures that you as a teacher have developed for the classroom.
4. Parents need to become acquainted with their child's accomplishments in school. Develop a communication system for all students. A second, more personal system may need to be developed for the student who is reluctant in following the rules that have been developed.
5. After becoming aware of the students potential, share that capability with the parents. It may be necessary at times to work with parents so they do not pressure the child beyond his/her individual potential. The opposite can also be true if the child is not working up to their potential.
6. Be personal but professional with parents. When communicating with the teacher, parents need to have a respect for the professional and know that the teacher cares about their child.
7. When sending written communications home to parents, share those ideas with a co-worker to assure yourself that you are on target. Let a co - worker read the communication for grammar and spelling.
8. Develop a web site and let parents know how to access it. The web site can be very simple to one with many bells and buttons. Whatever the case may be web sites are free in many locations on the Internet. You can place your class rules, expectations and long/short term assignments. Changing the web site on a weekly or daily bases with create interest for both parents and students. Make sure your web site is of a positive nature. If your not a computer "nerd" there are programs free to teachers to prepare a web site.

PARENT INVOLVEMENT

Parents must accept equal responsibility in helping solve the student's discipline problems. Unfortunately many parents are so involved emotionally with their children they cease to function in a positive, firm, and consistent manner. This type of parent often needs suggestions so he/she may view the child objectively.

Being a parent does not automatically provide wisdom and understanding. Wisdom and understanding comes from experience and learning from one's mistakes. The majority of parents raise well-discipline children. The educator must also be cognizant of the parent that is manipulated by his/her child. Educators in this real life situation should work toward educating these parents or directing them to professionals who can provide them with the skills necessary to work with their children.

Parents, like the classroom teacher and administrators, must work closely with the school and community to develop and solve student discipline problems.

WORKING WITH PARENTS

There are a number of opportunities that the classroom teacher and the school can provide to the parent when promoting and developing positive effective discipline.

Schools can provide workshops for parents, especially to those parents whose children are discipline problems. Workshops can address the issues that face the parent as well as the school. These issues include self-discipline, responsibility, problem solving, and self-esteem. (See section on developing parental workshops.)

Parents can work with teachers, support staff, and administrators in finding meaningful ways to implement social reinforces such as praising words, phrase expressions and the appropriate type of physical contact. In addition activity reinforces can be discussed with parents helping them decide when and how to use or not to use these reinforces. (See appendix Reinforces.)

PARENT CONFERENCES

Parent conferences can take many forms. It is important that the classroom teacher realizes that a conference can be held at anytime throughout the school year. The teacher does not need to wait until the formal scheduled conferences that are set by the school administration. Individual conferences, whether they be face to face or by telephone are often more effective, especially when held in a timely manner. Conferences tell the teacher a great deal about the child, as children often mirror their parents. Conferences tell the parents a great deal about the teacher as well. Therefore it is extremely important that these avenues of communication be well thought out and is as productive, friendly, positive and professional as possible.

When communicating with parents' simple guidelines can be used to strengthen the productivity of the conference and enhance the communication between parent and teacher.

1. Know the student. Parents are impressed with a teacher who knows their child and will accept the statements of the teacher when the educator knows both the positive and negative aspects of the student.
2. Talk about their child as if they were your only student, leaving other students out of the conversation, if at all possible.
3. Approach the conference with a positive attitude and confidence in yourself, just as you approach the students in your classroom. If you are confident there is no need to place the blame on other co-workers or past experiences the child may have had.
4. Listen and ask for suggestions. If a parent has a complaint, be willing to hear their point of view and share with them a willingness to address the complaint in a professional manner.
5. Be prepared for the conference by doing some pre-planning. Have suggestions and alternative suggestions ready to offer the parent. Avoid becoming defensive when the parent does not agree with your suggestions.

6. In your discussion, compare the behavior of the student in school with their cooperation and behavior at home. What technique does the parent's use at home that are effective and might also be incorporated in the classroom setting?
7. Remember that when you criticize the child you are also criticizing the parent. In most cases the parent will take the criticism in a personal manner and become defensive.
8. Give parents a choice in possible solutions. As teachers we are unfamiliar with the home environment. What may work in one family may be devastating to another.
9. Set the parents at ease. Sit at a table or in a chair next to the parent avoiding barriers such as the teacher's desk. Remember, the parent is the prime educator and is in a partnership with you as the teacher. That partnership must be emphasized by the educator and understood by the parent.
10. Statements should be of a positive nature: John can do more in controlling his behavior. He does know how to do the right thing.

WRITTEN COMMUNICATION

In today's hectic world, and with the demands that are placed on the educator, it is not often possible to have a conference with the parent. It is important that the educator keep the lines of communication open at all times and be punctual in dealing with problems that occur in the classroom. Written communication is one way of keeping parents informed and involved in the student's educational program. When using written communication it is important to be aware of a few essential elements. In doing so, the teacher's time will be well spent and hopefully the purposes intended will be achieved.

The following will be helpful in developing good communication when writing to parents:

1. Have a single purpose in mind; if your written communication covers too broad a field of topics the importance of your original intent will be lost.
2. State the substance of your letter in the first sentence. Parents are busy also. You can give details and reasons further on in the communication.
3. Write, as you would talk to the individual. Stay away from educational jargon and cluttered educational terminology. Use well-structure, correct punctuation and spelling. Remember, that parents are evaluating you by your writing.
4. Use the student's name, avoiding pronouns that can give a feeling of negativism.
5. Limit your sentences to no more than a dozen words.
6. Parents do not want to read a biography, keep your communication to one page if possible.
7. Be considerate of appearance. Type the letter if your handwriting is not legible.
8. Send copies of your letter, if necessary, to the principal or other co-workers who are involved with the student, but be selective.
9. Conclude your letter with a few positive statements.
10. Link your concerns to those of the school and the standards that you have developed in your discipline plan.
11. Be honest, factual and timely.

SUMMARY

Many parents have minimal problems with behavior at home or at school. The experience that teachers and parents have with misbehavior often results from the fact that children soon learn when an action, if any, will be taken either at home or school. Children learn that they can manipulate their parents and/or teachers. Working with parents in a personal and cooperative effort can effectively overcome the child's habits of misbehavior. Parents and teachers through word, example, and action must clearly demonstrate to the student that they are in charge. Children react in a positive manner to a positive, consistent discipline approach.

Teachers cannot discipline alone, and working with parents is an essential part of the ongoing discipline process. When the child has an understanding that the school and home are working together in a cooperative manner goals are achieved and can be maintained throughout the school year.

Remember that any communication with parents provide a picture of you as an educator. It can be a very positive tool. If you do not speak in complete organized sentences and write in an educated manner, it will be picked up by the parent and come back to hunt you as an educator. Many administrators require a copy of all written communication sent from the school. A good rule of thumb is to have another teacher proof all written forms of communication.

CHAPTER EIGHT

POSSIBLE PROBLEMS/SOLUTIONS

The following situations are provided as examples of various discipline problems that may occur in the classroom on a regular basis. With each problem suggestions are made that might correct the discipline problem.

There is no solution that will work in every case, nor is they're a archetype solution that can be used with every child. As stated earlier in the text each school and district has its own unique policies, which must be followed. Each school is unique just as each child is unique. Thus the solutions are only general in nature and are given as a possible technique that might be a beginning or foundation in managing the discipline problem.

THE ANGRY CHILD

Before looking at specific behavior problems that may occur in the classroom it would be beneficial to discuss the general category of the angry child. This child often times does not "fit" within any specific behavior problem as anger itself is the underlining factor for poor behavior and classroom discipline. (National Journal of Mental Health, Plane Talk Series) indicates the following:

Handling a student's anger can be puzzling, draining and distressing for adults. One of the major problems in dealing with anger in children is the angry feeling that is often stirred up in us. It has been said that we as parents, teachers, counselors and administrators need to remind ourselves that we were not always taught hot to deal with anger as a fact of life during our own childhood. We were led to believe that to be angry was to be bad, and we were often made to feel guilty for expressing anger.

It is easier to deal with a students' anger if we get rid of this notion. Our goal is not to repress or destroy angry feelings in students or in us, but rather to accept the feelings and to help channel and direct them to constructive ends.

Teachers must allow children to feel all their feelings. Adult skills can then be directed toward showing children acceptable ways of expressing their feelings. Strong feelings cannot be denied and angry outbursts should always be viewed as a sign of serious problems; they should be recognized and treated with respect.

To respond effectively to overly aggressive behavior in children we need to have some ideas about what may have triggered an outburst. Anger may be a defense to avoid painful feelings; it may be associated with failure, low self-esteem and feelings of isolation; or it may be related to anxiety about situations over which the child has no self-control.

Angry defiance may also be associated with feelings or dependency, and anger may be associated with sadness and depression. In childhood, anger and sadness are close to one another and it is important to remember that a child as anger expresses much of what an adult experiences as sadness.

When dealing with the angry child there is a number of concepts that the educator should follow.

1. Catch the child being good and following directions. Inform the child that you are pleased with his or her behavior. Using positive statements (See Chapter 9) can be an effective and lasting reinforcement for the child.

2. Deliberately ignore inappropriate behavior that can be tolerated. This doesn't mean however that you ignore the child or his behavior.
3. Provide physical outlets and other alternatives for the student. Sometimes the rules and regulations can be to confining for the angry child.
4. Express interests in the child; let them know that you are interested in them. Move closer to the child in order to curb their anger and its manifestations.
5. Ease tension through humor if possible. More anger on the part of the educator will magnify the anger in the child.
6. Appeal directly to the student. Take the time to communicate with the child and seek out the reason for the anger that exists within the child. Appeal to the child, letting them knows that you care, however that the anger that they are showing is not acceptable in the educational setting.
7. Make up your mind that you can say **NO** to the child. Sometimes it will be necessary to use physical restraint. Depending upon the age of the student, physical restraint should be used with caution and with a feeling of caring and understanding. It is difficult, if not impossible, to use physical restraint with students at the junior or senior high school level. Another group of students where physical restraint may not want to be used are those with special disabilities.
8. Work on the child's self-esteem. A child with a high level of self-esteem will have his or her anger under control a much greater portion of the time.

SPECIFIC BEHAVIORS / POSSIBLE SOLUTIONS

BEHAVIORS CONSIDERED

1. A student is disruptive during small group instruction time.
2. A student seems to be inattentive but performs well.
3. A student will not do his/her work.

4. Students are disorderly when standing in line.
5. Students are noisy or unruly when entering the classroom.
6. The student behaves incorrectly when other students receive praise or attention; cannot stand to lose in competition.
7. The student behaves in a manner that is inappropriate for a given situation such as: laughing at other students who make mistakes or become hurt.
8. Students are rude and have poor manners either with their classmates or the teacher.
9. The student refuses to recognize the authority of the teacher.
10. The student is impulsive in his behavior.
11. The student is consistent in not following the rules established for either the classroom or school.
12. The student is a constant talker and leads others to converse at inappropriate times.
13. The student is openly defiant to the teacher.
14. The student cheats in class by copying the work of other students in the class.
15. The student, although capable, refuses to do the assigned work.
16. The student is hyperactive and refuses to settle down in the classroom.
17. The student uses foul or unacceptable language in the classroom.
18. The student steals from the classroom or from other students.
19. Students are involved in fights with other students.

BEHAVIOR 1

A student is disruptive during small group instruction time.

1. Stop and remind the student of the rules.
2. Gesture to the student, indicating your need for the disruption to stop.

3. Depending on the age of the student, you may simply want to touch the student lightly on the arm and indicate your displeasure.
4. Praise the student who is behaving in a positive manner.
5. Stand by the student without commenting on the behavior.
6. Remove the student from the group, isolating him/her and simply state that they can return when they are ready to behave.

BEHAVIOR 2

A student seems to be inattentive but performs well.

1. Analysis the situation. Is it due to peer pressure?
2. If the student performs well on tests, work sheets and answers when called upon leave the student alone.
3. Speak with the student on an individual basis sharing your concern about the in attentiveness.

BEHAVIOR 3

A student will not do his/her work.

1. Check to see if the student has the ability to complete this particular level of work. If they do not have the ability adjust the assignment.
2. Stop and remind the student of the rules regarding the a action or situation
3. Remind them of the consequences that were established and discussed regarding incomplete work.
4. Put the student on a tape recorder where the work must be completed within a specific time setting.
5. Use a timer with the student.
6. Use a monitor (adult) teacher aide to work with the student.
7. Praise those who complete the work on time.

8. Discuss the problem with the student's parents in writing, by telephone or conference seeking suggestions.
9. Take away certain privileges until work is done.
10. Develop a contract.

BEHAVIOR 4

Students are disorderly when standing in line.

1. Remind them of the rules and consequences.
2. Praise those students who behave correctly.
3. Have them return to the classroom and line up by rows.
4. Share with them how they appear to others; approach their sense of pride.
5. Remove the student or reduce the amount of time the student is allowed to participate in a specific activity

BEHAVIOR 5

Students are noisy or unruly when entering the classroom.

1. Develop an assignment to be completed within the first few minutes of the class period. Give credit for completion.
2. Move about the room when the students are entering.
3. Face the students as they enter the room.
4. Remind them of the rules.
5. Provide them a short period of time to visit at the end of the class period. Set definite time limits.
6. Praise those students who follow the rules.
7. Develop a reward system for appropriate behavior but work toward reducing or eliminating the reward all together
8. Drop a thank you note to a student who has shown Improvement. Be prepared for the students by having materials ready at the beginning of the class.

BEHAVIOR 6

The student behaves incorrectly when other students receive praise or attention, cannot stand to lose in competition.

1. Reinforce the student when he/she does behave appropriately.
2. Give the student a tangible reward or an intangible reward such as a handshake, pat on the back when he/she behaves appropriately.
3. Speak to the student about the behavior in a private setting.
4. Write a contract spelling out the objectives for appropriate behavior.
5. Communicate with parents or co-workers regarding the problem for suggestions and support.
6. Identify a peer to act as a role model and mentor.
7. Do not allow the student to participate if the activity is to stimulating. Help the student obtain a level of success in an activity that can be mastered.

BEHAVIOR 7

The student behaves in a manner that is inappropriate for a given situation such as laughing at other students who make mistakes or become hurt.

1. Reinforce other students who act with appropriate behavior.
2. Speak with the student to make sure they understand what they are doing is unacceptable. Give reasons.
3. If you have not at an earlier time, stop and establish classroom rules and procedures for this type of behavior.
4. Reinforce the student for a change in behavior beginning with a small reward, gradually increasing the reward for long term-improved behavior.
5. Remove the student from the situation until he/she can demonstrate appropriate behavior. A time out corner may be

successful or by sending them to a co - worker who has agreed to work with you on the modification.
6. Modify or adjust situations that cause the student to behave in a negative manner.

BEHAVIOR 8

Students are rude and have poor manners either with their classmates or the teacher.

1. Determine if the behavior is the lack of training at home or is an attention getter device.
2. Identify the student's favorite classes and the reasons why.
3. Ignore the behavior and praise those in the classroom who act appropriately.
4. Discuss the behavior with the student in a private setting.
5. Develop a contract with rewards for a change in behavior.
6. Communicate with parents for recommendations and support.
7. Discuss the problem with co - workers for suggestions.
8. Limit the student's involvement in classroom activities if behaviors are inappropriate. Students should be aware of Consequences that lie ahead of them.
9. Redefine the classroom rules and procedures with the student.
10. Develop a peer relationship for the student so as to provide a model for appropriate behavior.

BEHAVIOR 9

The student refuses to recognize the authority of the teacher.

1. Determine what the student's home life is like and if the student's problems parallel parental authority.
2. The teacher should evaluate his/her relationship with the student making sure that they are secure in their role as teacher/student, rather than a friend of the student.

3. Be consistent with directions and adhere to the rules established at all times.
4. Discuss the problem with the student in a private conference.
5. Communicate with the parents for suggestions and support.
6. Develop a contract with the student.
7. Praise students who respect authority.
8. Develop a reward system for respect.
9. Remove privileges for students who do not accept the authority of the teacher in the classroom.

BEHAVIOR 10

The student is impulsive in his behavior.

1. Provide reinforces for the student for acting in a deliberated and responsive manner.
2. Speak with the student so he is aware of what he is doing that is not acceptable.
3. Reinforce students who are following the classroom rules and procedures.
4. Write a contract setting expectations for the student.
5. Notify parents of the problem for ideas and support.
6. Reduce the opportunity for impulsive behavior by limiting the decision making process.
7. Maintain supervision of the student at all times within the school environment.
8. Speak and work with the school counselor and other school support personnel.
9. Give the student additional responsibilities in the classroom.
10. Emphasize individual success or progress whenever possible.
11. Limit the student's access to the entire classroom.
12. Maintain consistency in the student's daily routines.

BEHAVIOR 11

The student is consistent in not following the rules established for either the classroom or school.

1. Determine, if possible, what expectations are required of the child at home. Parents often blame this behavior on everyone but themselves.
2. Keep good records of the student's behavior over a specific length of time.
3. Communicate both in writing and in person with the parents
4. Work to place the child in the most restricted environment possible.
5. Move the student to a location in the classroom where the teacher's presence can be felt at all times.
6. Develop a contract with the student to outlining expectations and build in rewards and/or Consequences.
7. Be consistent with the student demanding more of the child than other students in the classroom.
8. Limit the activities of the student to those he/she can handle successfully. Expand the activities as a reward for improved behavior.
9. Look for alternative approaches within the school setting to isolate the student from the classroom.
10. Obtain the help and advice of specialists in the school.
11. Let the student know your expectations and that you are concerned about him.
12. Set aside time for regular and timely one-on-one conferences with the student.
13. Praise the student for following the rules no matter how insignificant.
14. Work out a positive reinforcement plan with the parents that are reasonable and acceptable. Follow through with follow-up conferences and evaluation of the devised plan.

BEHAVIOR 12

The student is a constant talker and leads other to converse at inappropriate times.

1. Keep a " time out" chair in the classroom near your desk. If the student cannot stop talking they are assigned to the " time out " chair.
2. Ask questions of the talker that they are forced to answer. Phrase the questions so that the answer requires a response other than a yes or no answer.
3. Use facial expressions that carry a measure of displeasure on your part. Make sure the talker understands your displeasure.
4. If the student is a serious offender, offer a choice of punishments. Follow through with the consequences that you have developed with the class.
5. Appeal to their masculine or famine instincts. The student often responds to this treatment as they wish to me mucho in the eyes of their classmates. Use peer pressure to your advantage.
6. Use nonverbal communication. Move about the classroom to the location of the talker. Make your presence known.

BEHAVIOR 13

The student is openly defiant to the teacher.

1. If possible ignore the first occurrence, hopefully making the student realize that the action is not going to affect you or the class.
2. If the offence occurs again try isolating the student. Placing them in a location where they cannot see or receive reinforcement from the class.

3. Make a notation in your record book or somewhere that will help you keep an account of the action. The student should be fully aware of your notation.
4. Keep the rest of the class working while you talk to the student privately. Insist that the behavior be stopped and that you will not accept this type of behavior in the future.
5. After a period of time has passed, try to figure out what is causing the behavior and speak to the student about it.
6. As this type of behavior is unacceptable, the child who cannot change their behavior should be sent to the office for behavior modification.

BEHAVIOR 14

The student cheats in class by copying the work of other students in the class.

1. Discuss the need for honesty with the class, emphasizing that tests and quizzes are a means for the teacher to determine what the student has learned and a major function is to provide knowledge to the teacher for the purposes of retouching.
2. Inform students that you respect them for putting forth their best effort, not for the score that receive on a test or quiz.
3. When you discover a specific student has cheated emphasize the behavior with the student, not the result of their test score.
4. Don't embarrass or humiliate the student. Speak to the student on a one-to-one basis.
5. After you have spoken to the cheater, consider the situation closed. Don't bring it up again unless the cheating continues.

BEHAVIOR 15

The student, although capable, refuses to do the assigned work.

1. Avoid confrontation with the student while rewarding cooperative behavior wherever possible.
2. Focus on situations where the pupil shows an interest. Use praise for work that is totally or partially completed.
3. Reduce your criteria for the correctness of the task at the beginning, gradually increasing your expectations according to the ability of the student.
4. Wherever possible give the student a feeling of success. A token reward system or contract may be helpful once the child has begun completing the work.
5. Contact the parent to determine reasons why the student does not complete the work assigned.

BEHAVIOR 16

The student is hyperactive and refuses to settle down in the classroom.

1. Provide as much structure for the student as possible. Make classroom rules and procedures as consistent as possible for the student on a day to day basis.
2. Minimize directions for the student, as the hyperactive child is sensitive to all kinds of stimuli.
3. Couple verbal messages with visual clues to reinforce a message to the student.
4. Use colored paper, visuals to focus the student's attention on the task.
5. Set up a quiet corner or location in the classroom where the child can refocus for a brief period of time.

6. Develop learning - behavioral plan with the student that the child and teacher can live with. The plan should contain rewards and consequences for the action of the student.

BEHAVIOR 17

The student uses foul or unacceptable language in the classroom.

1. Indicate to the student in a calm manner that the language that is being used is unacceptable in the classroom or school setting.
2. Remember students repeat what they hear in their environment. Keeping this in mind, if the language continues, contacting the home may be an important factor to eliminate the unacceptable behavior.
3. If it is an isolate occurrence, keep a record of the outburst, and try to adjust the language by speaking privately with the student.
4. Don't ask the student to apologize to the class. Students will be aware of the language and that it is unacceptable.
5. Don't take foul language as a personal offense, but rather one against the class or school.
6. For older student, speak to them about developing words that are expletives and ask them, if they must, to use them in place of foul language.
7. Do not abdicate your responsibility by turning a deaf ear. Foul language is unacceptable and the student needs to be aware of the fact that you will not accept it in the classroom.

BEHAVIOR 18

The student steals from the classroom or from other students.

1. Students who steal do not wish other to be aware of their action. Speak with the student and inform them that they must return the item. Inform the student that further occurrence will result in others being informed of their action.
2. If something of value is missing give the culprit a chance to return the article immediately without penalty. Designate a location for the items return.
3. If the item(s) are not returned within the time limits set send a referral form to the administration. Stealing cannot be tolerated. Keep the class, if possible, until a member of the administration comes to the room.
   - After a stealing situation has been resolved give the student an opportunity to be trusted.

BEHAVIOR 19

Fighting Between Students. Fighting between students occurs for various reasons. It occurs in most educational settings. The teacher should assume the responsibility of being a mediator for those involved.

1. Fighting cannot be tolerated in any setting. The teacher should escort those involved in the fight to the office for administrative discipline action.
2. When the fight breaks out, separate those involved in the confrontation. Speak to the students firmly and briefly. Do not take sides.
3. Talk to each student or group separately. After a cooling off period, the two students or groups can be brought together to discuss their differences.

4. When appropriate, and at the proper time, a discussion of behavior and the right way to solve differences should be addressed with the class.

DISCIPLINE OPTIONS

After you have developed and taught your goals and objectives the students can be reminded of what the expectations for the classroom are and the need to adhere to them. Options that may be considered when working with students might include, but are not limited to the following.

1. Give a positive statement to the student to stop and action that is not acceptable.
2. Increasing responsibility helps some students.
3. Always be positive in your reinforcement. Negativism brings about negative reactions.
4. Behavior contracts are very effective with some students.
5. Isolation of the student from other students can be helpful.
6. Writing out the behavior with possible solutions by the teacher and student sitting down together can be effective as it develops awareness of a problem.
7. Try group solving problem activities after determining these problems, which ones need the greatest amount of attention.
8. Hold private conferences with the student.
9. Meet with co-workers who have developed an expertise in a specific field.
10. Develop responsibility charts, awards, or tokens.
11. Create a big brother, big sister concept.
12. Supervision by placing the child in the classroom where students are physically close to the teacher or an aide.
13. Reevaluate the classroom environment on a regular basis.
14. Obtain parent involvement, through conferences, written communication, classroom visitations and parental ownership.

15. Develop teacher stature and consistency; evaluate your progress on regular bases. You can't change what you don't acknowledge. Don't be afraid to make those changes.
16. Supervisor involvement is essential for support and developing creative ideas, when asking for this involvement use it as questioning process not as a deficiency on your part.
17. There should be humor in the classroom on a daily bases.
18. Suggestions boxes and other techniques, which serve the same purpose, are helpful to obtain student ideas and feelings about their classroom environment.
19. Positive reinforcement through the caring process will result in positive results.

SUMMARY

The above behaviors are only a sampling of problems that occur in the classroom. To include all that exist would constitute another book in itself. These behaviors are provided as examples with possible solutions. Solutions may vary with the student's age and maturity. The solutions suggested could be applied to most discipline problems depending upon the age of the student, level of maturity and how frequent they are implemented.

CHAPTER NINE

PARENT INVOLVEMENT – START EARLY

Parent Involvement is extremely important in any child's education and as we all know the earlier the parent becomes involved with the process the more beneficial it is to the child. This involvement covers a married of experiences during the child's education. As children grow older they are less likely to want their parents involved in their educational setting. This is especially noted during the junior high school years and continues through high school. An exception, of course, is parent involvement in sports activities and archenemy contests. However, we see that when these activities come to an end parents are not encouraged by their children to participate in the activities that take place in the classroom on a daily bases.

Research shows that parent involvement is related to student achievement. Research also shows that parents of low socio-economic status tend to have a harder time getting involved in their child's education. Thus student achievement is implausible. In order to raise the expectations of those failing students, the parents must be educated on how to communicate with the school, become involved, educate the child at home and how to instigate learning through the summer months.

Therefore, it is in the school districts best interest to implement a parent education curriculum to improve school environment and community. Because most parents work, it is hard to find time to improve on their own education let alone improve a parent/school relationship. A parent education program should take place over a short semester and meet one night a week to ensure enrollment. Class periods would be limited to three hours a night or less. The length of the class should be such as to ensure the parent the importance of the subject matter and make it worth while for them to interrupt there evening.

Parent Education for Successful Involvement in Schools and at Home would focus on not only parent improvement, but also transfers to the student and the feeling of self-worth. Once a parent shows true involvement with a child, that child will grow academically and socially.

Parent education is becoming more and more necessary. A child needs to have their parent's involved with their education. The parent may want to, but they don't know how to attain the knowledge in order to become actively involved. Through parent education, they can.

There is a great need for developing a course for parents where they can come together with school personal and other parents. This coming together will allow parents to see that they and their children have the same hopes, fears and frustrations as many of the other parents within the school environment. Doing this and participating in a course for parents should be held at the elementary level for reasons stated earlier in this chapter.

Research has shown the importance of parent involvement in their children's' lives to be very effective for student achievement. Lazar (1978) found through a long-term study that low-income parents who become actively involved with their children perform better in school. He also discovered that there are less special education placements in involved families. A literature review led by Henderson and Berla (1994) found that when parents are involved, their children do better in school and that school they attend also does better. Becher (1984) concluded that parent education programs which train low-income parents to work with their children and schools are effective in improving a child's language skills, improve test taking, and improve a child's behavior in school.

Parent involvement builds self-confidence; therefore it improves student achievement. Stearns and Paterson (1973) came up with a chain graph to link a parental role with the academic improvement of a child. **Stearns and Paterson graphic (1973)**

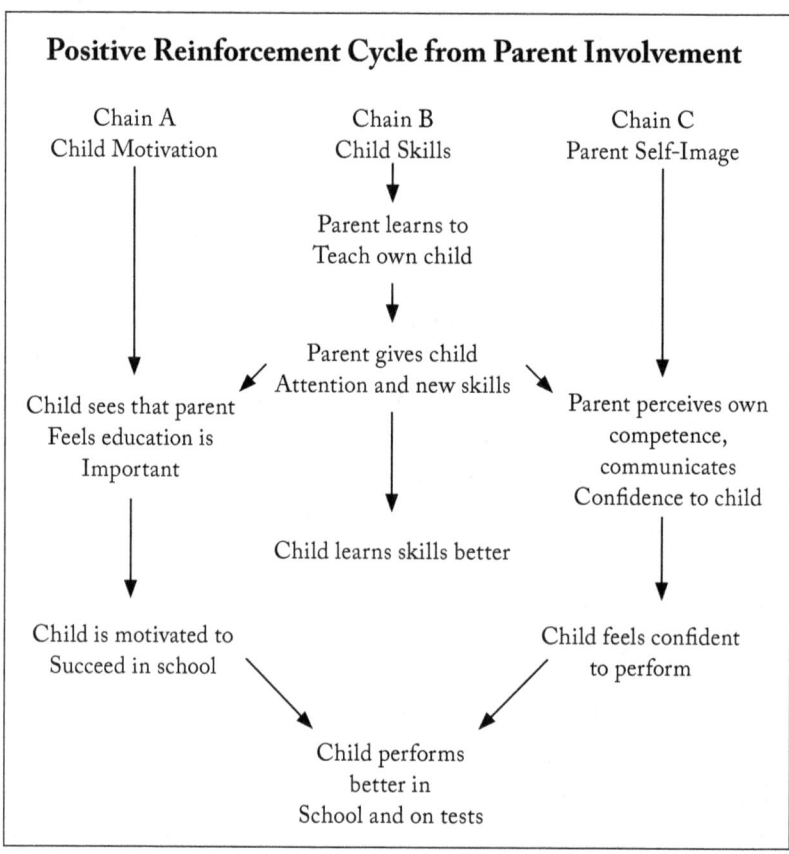

As stated earlier, it is easier to get parents' involved when their children are at the elementary. Although this may be true the last few years have indicated the need for parents to become and stay involved at the secondary level. Educators may choose to set up a one evening study session for parent's choosing different nights so that all parent's can attend. This study session should cover a variety of topics.

The topics might include the following:

- Homework and the necessity for it
- The need to have assignments completed.
- School philosophy
- Discipline at school
- Bulling in the school and a policy to reduce its effect on students
- The need for parental involvement
- What to look for in their children that might be a change in habits
- Any additional topics unique to the local school

No matter what plan or scheme is designed every effort is a step in the right directions. Make it easy for parents to become involved. Show parents the need and give them good reasons for becoming involved. YOU HAVE TO BE A SALESPERSON.

(See chapter 12 for a simple lesson plan)

There are a number of educational instructions and states that offer information for teaching of parents.

(See chapter 12 for a simple lesson plan)

Chapter Ten

SUMMARY

Discipline in the classroom is an extremely complex variable which, when carried out in an organized and consistent manner, can provide the classroom teacher an environment that is enjoyable and conducive to learning.

In any social situation, people are unsure as to the restraints under which they are to operate. Students are no different, and they must be taught behaviors that are acceptable for the classroom. In teaching the appropriate behaviors the teacher must consider that some of the discipline problems arise out of an academic base while others are due to peer relationships, environmental and cultural factors outside of the school. All in all most Students are conformists; they fear being different and even the best students will engage in inappropriate activities. It is the teacher's responsibility to work with the student as an individual as well as with the students as a group.

Teachers will enjoy teaching when the majority of their time does not have to be spent on discipline problems. Start out with well-planned goals and objective; be willing to revise them as the need arises. Be confident in one's own unique ability and let students know that you are consistent and caring. We might say is true about classroom management and organization. There is no separating the three elements in the classroom. Each element plays a unique part in the days activities. A well run classroom develops appropriate discipline procedures only if there is good organization and management. No one, no matter how educated, how many degrees in education has the complete answer to the topics presented in this text. We can only try different methods, take suggestions Today, because of the critical need in dealing with a wide range of concerns many school districts are experimenting and /or implementing new programs to consider the students, parents and the districts needs.

GUIDELINES

A few simple guidelines can be helpful to new teachers entering the classroom for the first time as well as veteran teachers. They might look like the following.
- Don't take yourself too seriously.
- Don't listen to other teachers' evaluations of student, form your own opinions. Students can change too.
- Prepare twice as much material as you think you will need.
- Start off each class/day well organized, having something planned for the students as soon as they enter the room.
- Be yourself, students need to know you are human. Students need someone to look up to; they have friends, there is a difference.
- Be aware of your personal moods, feelings and how they \ affect your classroom environment.
- Don't overreact to situations. Take time to think thing through so that you do not have to make changes or find you cannot follow through on what you have said.
- Be enthusiastic about your subject area.
- Have fun; remember teaching is one of the helping professions.
- Hold your students to high standards; they will appreciate you for it in the long run.
- Let students know you care about them and that you will find time to help and listen to their individual needs.
- Treat the students, as you would want to be treated by you fellow teachers, administrators and parents.

- You are part of a team; enlist the help of administration, parents and co-workers.
- Parents are teachers also. Their enthusiasm and cooperation is essential to good discipline. Seek their support and advise as it pertains to their children.
- Getting off to the right start is critical in developing good discipline in the classroom. If your discipline has fallen short of your expectations then stop and reevaluate, reorganize, replan and reemploy, for each day in the classroom can be a new beginning where good discipline and good instruction go hand in hand.

CHAPTER ELEVEN

USEABLE FORMS AND IDEAS

A. A MODEL FOR REACHING AGREEMENT IN CONFLICT
B. REWARD ALTERNATIVES
C. SHORT AND LONG TERM REWARD CHART
D. CONTRACTS
E. RECOGNIZING STUDENTS THROUGH PRAISE
F. SELF EVALUATION AS A ROLE MODEL
G. SELF ASSESSMENT AS A HAPPY TEACHER
H. WHAT IS YOUR ENTHUSIASM RATING
I. A TEACHER'S SELF EVALUATION
J. CLASSROOM MANAGEMENT CHECKLIST
K. CLASSROOM RULES
L. IMPLEMENTATION PLAN FOR CLASSROOM RULES
M. A CHECKLIST FOR WORKING WITH ADMINISTRATION AND CO-WORKERS
N. CLASSROOM QUESTIONS/WHAT KIND
O. BEHAVIOR REPORT
P. TEN DIRECTIVES OF GOOD DISCIPLINE
Q. WORK SHEET FOR SELF - ESTEEM
R. TIME LOG
S. 5 STEPS TO PROBLEM SOLVING

T. DISCIPLINE CARD
U. Getting To Know You Activates
V. Class Meeting Samples
W. Student Conference Form
X. Dr. Phil's Anti Bulling Pledge

SAMPLE A

A MODEL FOR REACHING AGREEMENT IN CONFLICT

Conflicts arise often between teacher, parent, student, co-workers and administrators. The authors intend in this model is to provide a means to resolve conflict so all feel satisfied with the outcomes.

1. Prepare yourself; look at various options prior to setting down with others to resolve the conflict.
2. Determine what the common goals are that you have with the other person. Capitalize on these goals.
3. State your need, or problem, **NOT** your position. Give well though out reasons for your position or need.
4. Find out the needs of the other person. What can you give to them in return for helping you meet your needs?
5. Look at various problem-solving techniques. What alternatives might be agreed upon? Are you willing to listen and look at alternatives?
6. When agreement has been reached, what methods of follow through will be used and who will be responsible for them?

GRADE YOURSELF ON YOUR
AGREEMENT REACHING SKILLS

HOW WELL DID YOU DO?

Excellent - Good - Fair - Poor

Areas that need improvement ... (List)
Areas that are satisfactory ... (List

SAMPLE B

REWARD ALTERNATIVES

Students who display appropriate behavior need to achieve recognition. One way of providing recognition is through a reward alternative. The following list can provide the teacher with ideas that might afford a successful level of encouragement to the student.

REWARDS

Stars	Food
Chips/tokens	Punch
Stickers, seals	Point chart
Outdoor lessons	Library passes
cards	Singing
Use of school equipment	Note to parents
Verbal approval	Choices in game play
Awards-weekly, monthly	Ink stamps
Use of school	Equipment Tickets
Free Time	Assisting Others
Lunch with teacher	Class leader for a day
Added classroom responsibilities	Classroom Privileges
Tutor another student	Class leader for a day

SAMPLE C

SHORT AND LONG TERM REWARD CART

Student _____ Date_____

Desired Behavior(s) - list

_____
_____
_____
_____
_____
_____
_____
_____

Sort/Long Term Reward - list

_____
_____
_____
_____
_____
_____
_____
_____

SAMPLE D

CONTRACTS

Contracts should be a simple agreement between two or more individuals. When developing a contract the content should be realistic and achievable. Each party involved should understand clearly the reason for the contract and understand all elements contained in it.

SAMPLE CONTRACT

Date:_____

This contract is written and executed between _____

and _____.

Objective: _____

Length of time: _____

SPECIAL CONDITIONS

_____

_____

_____

I will fulfill the conditions of this contract as indicated above and agree to all conditions stated in the contract.

_____   _____

(Signatures)

SAMPLE CONTRACT - 2 (FOR YOUNGER STUDENTS)

	Excellent	Average	Needs Improvement
Monday			
Tuesday			
Wednesday			
Thursday			
Friday			

Length of time: Week, Month, or Year

I _____ will follow the rules and conditions of the contract as told to me.

REWARDS/CONDITIONS

_____

_____

_____

Date: _____

Teacher: _____

Student: _____

(Each day is checked in the appropriate column according to the behavior of the student)

SAMPLE E

RECOGNIZING STUDENTS THROUGH PRAISE

Students for the most part will respond in a much more favorable manner with praise than with admonishment. The following are words and phrases that the teacher can use to encourage students in the achievement of good behavior. All praise should be used with prudence and according to the age and maturity level of the individual student.

NON - VERBAL PRAISE

Smiling	acting surprised	winking
Showing interest	laughing	nodding head
Hand shakes	pat on head	hugging
Touching	holding hand	moving chair

VERBAL PRAISE - WORDS

Marvelous	groovy	sharp
Wow	unbelievable	excellent
Yes	best	O.K.
Nifty	cool	unique
Brave	fabulous	super
Delightful	brilliant	perfect

VERBAL PRAISE - PHRASES

I like that
You've got it now
You're working so hard
Go for it
You're thinking now
Keep it up
What neat work
I like what I see
Right on
Good thinking
That's a good point

You are getting so smart
That was outstanding
Looking good
I'm pleased
that's really neat
Good job
Congratulations?
Superior work
Far out
Neat paper/job
I'm proud of you

This list is limited only by the teacher's imagination.

SAMPLE F

SELF EVALUATION AS A ROLE MODEL

1. Superior (4 points) 2. Above Average (3 points) 3. Average (2 points) 4. Need Improvement (1 point)

Characteristic	Evaluation
Walk with dignity	_____
Gestures	_____
Use of Voice	_____
Use of speech	_____
Tempérament/Disposition	_____
Acceptante	_____
Scholarly	_____
Teaching of Subject	_____
School Awareness	_____
Maturity	_____
Communication	_____

Total Score: _____

44 points - Top score - Your great
33 points - You're doing an outstanding job
22 points - You're doing well, evaluate the low areas
11 points - There is room for improvement.

FROM CRISIS TO TRANQUILITY

MY IMPROVEMENT PLAN

_____
_____
_____
_____
_____
_____
_____
_____

My Target date and reevaluation date:

_____

_____

Target Date   Reevaluation Date

_____   _____

SAMPLE G

SELF-ASSESSMENT AS A HAPPY TEACHER

TRAIT ==	ALWAYS (5 PTS)	SOMETIMES (3 PTS)	SELDOM (1 PT)

CHARRATERISTIC	POINTS
A. I like to go to work in the morning	_____
B. I get to school early.	_____
C. I enjoy my students	_____
D. I love kid's	_____
E. I praise students frequently	_____
F. Student feel comfortable with me	_____
G. My lessons are interesting	_____
H. I like my co - workers	_____

TOTAL POINTTS _____

30 - 40 POINTS - EXCELLENT
20 - 29 POINTS - GOOD
10 - 19 POINTS - NEEDS EVALUATION OF CAREER

SAMPLE H

WHAT IS YOUR ENTHUSIASM RATING?

You can determine just how enthusiastic you are by using the eight enthusiasm behaviors. The most effective method would be to videotape one or two lessons and rate yourself. If a videotape recorder is not available, persuade a colleague (with a reciprocal agreement) to observe you.

A word of caution: Don't rely too heavily on the results of only one observation. Repeated observations will enable you and your observer to evaluate the level of enthusiasm. Try changing your low-enthusiasm performance to a higher level by practicing the behaviors below.

>Dull or unenthusiastic - 8-20 points
>Moderate level of enthusiasm - 21-42
>Very high level of enthusiasm - 43-56

SCALE

LOW		MEDIUM			HIGH	
1	2	3	4	5	6	7

1. Vocal Delivery

LOW

Monotone, minimum inflections, little variation in speech, poor articulation

MEDIUM

Pleasant variations of pitch, volume, and speed; good articulation.

HIGH

Great and sudden changes from rapid excited speech to a whisper; varied tone and pitch.

2. Eyes

LOW

Looked dull or bored; seldom opened eyes wide or raised eyebrows; avoids eye contact; often maintains a blank stare.

MEDIUM

Appeared interested: occasionally lighting up, shining, and opening wide.

HIGH

Characterized as dancing, snapping, shining, lighting up frequently, opening wide, eyebrows raised; maintains eye contact while avoiding staring.

3. Gestures

LOW

Seldom moved arms out toward person or object; never used sweeping movements; kept arms at side or folded, rigid.

MEDIUM

Often pointed, occasional sweeping motion using body, head, arms, hands, and face; maintained steady pace of gesturing.

HIGH

Quick and demonstrative movements of body, head, arms, hands, and face.

4. *Body Movement*

LOW

Seldom moved from one spot, or from sitting to standing position; sometimes "paces" nervously.

MEDIUM

Moved freely, slowly, and steadily.

HIGH

Large body movements, swung around, walked rapidly, changed pace; unpredictable and energetic; natural body movements.

5. *Facial Expressions*

LOW

Appeared deadpan, expressionless or frowned; little smiling; lips closed.

MEDIUM

Agreeable; smiled frequently; looked pleased, happy, or sad if situation called for.

HIGH

Appeared vibrant, demonstrative; showed many expressions; broad mile; quick, sudden changes in expression.

6. *Word Selection*

LOW

Mostly nouns, few descriptions or adjectives; simple or trite expressions.

MEDIUM

some descriptions or adjectives or repetition of the same ones.

HIGH

Highly descriptive, many adjectives, great variety.

7. *Acceptance of Ideas and Feelings*

LOW

Little indication of acceptance or encouragement; may ignore students' feelings or ideas.

MEDIUM

Accepted ideas and feelings; praised or clarified; some variations in response, but frequently repeated same ones.

HIGH

Quick to accept, praise, encourage, or clarify; many variations in response; vigorous nodding of head when agreeing.

7. Overall Energy Level

LOW

Lethargic; appears inactive, dull, or sluggish.

MEDIUM

Appeared energetic and demonstrative sometimes, but mostly maintained an even level.

HIGH

Exuberant; high degree of energy and vitality; highly demonstrative.

<u>Score Summary:</u>
Area: 1. ___ 2. ___ 3. ___ 4. ___ 5. ___ 6. ___ 7. ___ 8. ___
Total Area Points: _____

- Developed by: Mary L. Collins, 1976 - Publisher Unknown.
-

SAMPLE I

A TEACHERS SELF EVALUATION

1. Were all students able to handle the work required?
2. Did I teach to mastery?
3. Was my instruction interesting and did student have a chance to achieve immediate feedback?
4. Did I praise students for correct behavior and responses?
5. Did I correct students mistakes in a positive manner?
6. Did I listen to students and was I aware of their needs?
7. Did I follow my lesson?
8. Was I well organized?
9. Was I consistent?
10. Did I plan extra work, if needed, and provide for individual differences in the assignments, class requirements?

SAMPLE J

CLASSROOM MANAGEMENT CHECKLIST

A) Achieved B) Achieved, but needs work
C) Not yet achieved.

CATEGORY	A	B	C
Classroom arrangement			
Student seating			
Daily Schedule			
Beginning activities			
Class Rules/Procedures			
Student participation			
Activities varied			
Work displayed			
Location of Teacher			
Teacher Desk			
Rest room procedures			
Transition procedures			
Handling class materials			
Small/large group activities			
Varied instruction techniques			
Positive reinforcement factor			
Consequences for poor behavior			
Teacher/Student self confidence			
Time on task			
Lessons complete and organized			
Balanced time structure for			

SARAH ROBINSON

Instruction and silent work _____

Number of areas ranked "A" _____ **"B"** _____ **"C"** _____

My self-evaluation

STRENGTHS:

_____
_____
_____
_____

AREAS NEEDING IMPROVEMENT:

_____
_____
_____
_____

SAMPLE K

MY CLASSROOM RULES

1. _____
_____

2. _____
_____

3. _____
_____

4. _____
_____

5. _____
_____

6. _____
_____

7. _____
_____

Comments/Suggestions:

SAMPLE L

IMPLEMENTATION PLAN FOR CLASSROOM RULES

_____

Rule # _____

Date of Implementation: _____

Who will implement: _____

Evaluate (date)_____ Result _____

Rule # _____

Date of Implementation: _____

Who will implement: _____

Evaluate (date)_____ Result _____

Rule # _____

Date of Implementation: _____

Who will implement: _____

Evaluate (date)_____ Result _____

Rule # _____

Date of Implementation: _____

Who will implement: _____

Evaluate (date)_____ Result _____

Rule # _____

Date of Implementation: _____

Who will implement: _____

Evaluate (date)_____ Result _____

Rule # _____

Date of Implementation: _____

Who will implement: _____

Evaluate (date)_____ Result _____

Rule # _____

Date of Implementation: _____

Who will implement: _____

Evaluate (date)_____ Result _____

Rule # _____

Date of Implementation: _____

Who will implement: _____

Evaluate (date)_____ Result _____

SAMPLE M

A CHECKLIST FOR WORKING WITH ADMINISTRATION AND CO-WORKERS

Each school is unique as are the administration and staff that work within that educational setting. The following provides a general "rule of thumb "guide for working with others.

< **Ask yourself how you compare with the general guidelines.**>

1. Do I maintain my position of responsibility and leadership while being friendly and helpful?

2. Do I encourage teamwork?

3. Do I back others when they express their ideas?

4. Do I work to establish school wide goals in discipline?

5. Do I listen and try to understand the problems that others face each day in their role as educators?

6. Am I consistent and just in my requests when dealing with problem students?

7. Do I avoid the use of threats and ultimatums?

8. Can I laugh at myself when I make mistakes?

9. Can I share my discipline ideas with others and accept criticism of my ideas?

10. Am I open to suggestions and willing to try new ideas?

SAMPLE N

CLASSROOM QUESTIONS -WHAT KIND?

Well thought out questions provide the classroom teacher an opportunity to react with students in an organized manner. Good questioning techniques are an essential part of the discipline process.

CONCEPTS:
Traditionally, questions have been used to determine what knowledge has been learned. To often isolated bits of knowledge of little value.

There is a wide range in quality of questions. Students can be led through all kinds of thinking through the use of questions.

MEMORY:
Memory, recall, is the lowest level of questioning. The student is not asked to compare/relate to or makes any inductive -deductive process on his own.

The instructor, presenter, scans the text or content materials to find facts and asks the students to remember the facts, often the inconsequential is emphasized.

Example: What is the religion of most people in Mexico?

COMPREHENSION AND INTERPRETATION:

Comprehension is the lowest level of understanding. Interpretation is what the students relate, fact, generalization, definitions, values and skills.

Questions may be comparisons as well as cause and effect relationships.

Example; why is it desirable to have the Congress approve all agreements with other countries?

APPLICATION:
This type of question gives students practice in the transfer of learning, i.e. using abstract knowledge in concrete situations.

Example: What are the possible future happenings if global warming continues

ANALYSIS:
Analysis questions require one to break down a situation into its basic elements or to solve a problem by the process of reasoning.

Example: If the rain forest continues to be destroyed, what do you think the next move of the worlds' nations will be?

SYNTHESIS:
The reverse of analysis is putting together elements to form a whole. Inductive reasoning from the specific to the general is involved.

These questions encourage students to engage in imaginative original thinking.

Example: Because the past methods of saving the ozone layer have not been effective, what different suggestions could be proposed?

EVALUATION:

Two main steps are:
1. Set up approximate standards or values.
2. Determine how closely these standards or values are met.

Evaluations can be used in subjective ways.

Example: Do you think that the present proposal for ending oil spills will terminate the problem or hasten the problem?

SUMMARY:

A teacher composes or selects questions for instruction and evaluation nearly every day. The more modest commitment to taxonomy would lead them to use the six basic kinds of questions while performing this normal function.

A reasonable rule of thumb is that a minimum of one-third of the time spent in questioning be devoted to questions above the memory level.

Good questions are hard to compose and some units lend themselves better to one type than another

To maximize good questioning/thinking the instructor must present subject matter from a variety of sources in addition to the printed materials.

MULTIPLE CHOICES:

1. Include a least four options.
2. Avoid phony choices.
3. Often use none or all.
4. Keep options grammatically consistent.

SUBJECTIVE (ESSAY)

1. A good question requires students to organize and express ideas in their own words.

2. Do not use essay questions to evaluate knowledge that could be tested with objective questions.

3. Have defined criteria for evaluating subjective questions.

4. Comments on essay questions are more revealing to the student than a single letter grade.

SHARING AND QUESTIONING ACTIVITY:

1. Vary your methods.
2. Have students serve as discussion leaders.
3. Have students evaluate other students.
4. Have the students develop questions that may be asked in a quiz situation.
5. Ask students to evaluate the topic (s).

As much of the classroom time is spent asking questions, good discipline depends on the quality of the question - answer process. Good, thought-provoking questions will enable the teacher to improve the discipline process in the classroom.

SAMPLE O

BEHAVIOR REPORT

Many schools have developed behavior reports for the teacher to use in communicating with the office or with parents. If one does not exist, the following may be useful.

Student _____ Date: _____

Teacher: _____ Telephone #_____

Reason for this report:

Good Points to be considered:
_____
_____
_____
_____

Areas of needed improvement:
_____
_____
_____
_____

— FROM CRISIS TO TRANQUILITY —

Recommendations:
Long or short term

_____
_____
_____
_____
_____

Parent comments:

_____
_____
_____
_____
_____

Signature of Teacher: _____

Signature of Parent: _____ Date: _____

SAMPLE P

TEN DIRECTIVES OF GOOD DISCIPLINE

1. Students are the purpose of my work.

2. Students are human beings who are deserving of my respect and understanding.

3. Students want and deserve consistency in their school environment.

4. Students have different abilities and come from various background and cultures. These must be considered in my teaching and discipline techniques.

5. Students need an understanding that I have feelings needs and goals.

6. An essential part of my classroom must be providing a secure and enjoyable place for students.

7. All students have a right to the best education that I can provide.

8. Students should have the opportunity to have ownership in their classroom organization and procedures.

9. Teaching is a cooperative effort between parents, students, and co-workers.

10. The better prepared that I am, as a teacher will result in a more effective learning and discipline environment.

SAMPLE Q

WORK SHEET FOR SELF-ESTEEM

Editors Note: The teacher can use this work sheet in a variety of ways depending upon the age and maturity of the individual child. Following the completion of the instrument discussion should take place so that the greatest benefit can be obtained from its content.

Directions: Complete each section as completely and honestly as possible.

Part 1. What is self-esteem? What does self-esteem mean to me?

_____
_____
_____
_____
_____
_____

List the "things" that make you feel good. (Happy, smart)

_____
_____
_____
_____
_____
_____

List the "things" that make you feel sad. (Bored, tired)
_____
_____
_____
_____
_____
_____
_____

Part 2. How does my self-esteem affect my life? In School
_____
_____
_____
_____
_____
_____
_____

At Home _____
_____
_____

With Friends _____
_____
_____

Someday your future career _____
_____
_____

Part 3. When do I make the changes I want to make to improve my self-esteem?
_____
_____
_____

How do I handle others:
_____
_____
_____

Who makes me feel good?
_____
_____
_____

Who makes me feel sad?
_____
_____
_____

What can I do to feel better about negative statements?
_____
_____
_____

Part 4. How do I deal with disappointments?
_____
_____
_____
_____

Part 5. What are my strengths? (good points)
_____
_____
_____
_____

Part 6. Who should I ask for help?
_____
_____
_____
_____

Part 7. What are my realistic goals?
_____
_____
_____
_____

Part 8. Who are my role models?
_____
_____
_____
_____

―――― FROM CRISIS TO TRANQUILITY ――――

FEEL GOOD!
I'M O.K. - YOUR O.K.

My name:_____

Date: _____

SAMPLE R

TIME LOG

Author's Note: Teaching is a time consuming process. The less time that is required on the daily discipline routines the more quality time will be left for the other required activities that are a normal part of the teachers daily schedule. This time log is provided so that the teacher can analyze where time is spent during the school day and where changes can be made.

Name_____ Week of_____

Item Variable   Monday Tuesday Wednesday Thursday Friday

		Monday	Tuesday	Wednesday	Thursday	Friday
1	Classroom Management Materials					
2	Discipline Problems					
3	Record Keeping					
4	Teaching Small Groups, 5-10					
5	Teaching the Entire Class					
6	Planning					
7	Interruptions					
8	Grading of Papers					

#	Task					
9	Managing Resources, People					
10	Scheduling					
11	Out of Class Response-abilities					
12	Emergencies					
13	Observing					
14	Monitoring					
15	Listening					
16	Talking					
17	Other					

Please record minutes per day/class spent on each of the above tasks; total and identify how you now spend most of your time. Determine where you need to make changes.

Totals: 1___ 2___ 3___ 4___ 5___ 6___ 7___ 8___ 9___
10___ 11___ 12___ 13___ 14___ 15___ 16___ 17___

SAMPLE S

5 STEPS TO PROBLEM SOLVING

I Introductions

1. Introduce yourself and ask the participants to state their names. Thank them for coming.
2. Explain that there are four rules that make mediation work.
   * Agree to try to solve the problem
   * No name-calling or physical fighting
   * Do not interrupt
   * Be as honest as you can
3. Ask each student if they agree to the rules.
4. Explain that everything said here is: CONFIDENTIAL except for information on drugs. Weapons or alcohol on school property or at school events.

II Listening to What Happened

1. Mediators decide who will go first.
2. Ask person # 1 for their story.
3. Repeat what you have heard, using Active Listening.
   * Restate the facts
   * Reflect their feelings
4. Ask them if you are correct.

Repeat steps 2-4 with person # 2

III Stating What Each Person Wants

1. If it's not clear yet, help each person figure out what they want.

   Ask more questions if there is anything you don't understand.

   Examples:

   Tell me more about...
   How long has this been going on?
   When did this happen?
   What would you like to see happen now?

   ### NO SOLUTIONS YET!

2. When you can, say to each person: "<u>#1</u>", it seems to me that you want _____. Is that right? Did I miss anything?

   "<u>#2</u>". It seems to me that you want _____. Is that right? Did I miss anything?

   ### <u>NOW</u> it's time to help them find solutions!

IV Finding Solutions

"What can they do about it?"

For now:

* Ask person # 1 "What can you do now to solve this?"

* Ask person # 2 "What can you do now to solve this?"

In the future.

>   * **Ask** person # 1 "What could you do differently in the future if the same problem arises?"

>   • Ask person # 2 " What could you do differently in the future if the same problem arises?"

Help students find a solution they both think is good.

>   * Is it specific? Does it tell when, who, how?

>   * Can each person do what he or she says they will?

>   * Did both disputants agree to something??

V   Wrap Up

1. To prevent rumors, ask each person to tell their friends that their conflict has been resolved.

2. Congratulate them.

3. Complete the report form.

4. After they leave, congratulate yourselves for the hard work.

SAMPLE T

THÉ DISCIPLINE CARD

When a student is a behavior problem for more than one teacher or staff member a Discipline Card can be a useful instrument for the positive change in behavior.

All staff members involved should meet to determine what rules and what is appropriate behavior for the individual child.

The student carries the card with him or her throughout the school day and has it available for each staff member they come in contact with that day.

The first time the student disrupts the classroom the staff member enters the infraction and initials the first consequence, the second time the second consequence and so on.

Since the student is a persistent behavior problem the first consequence on the card should not be a warning. If the student loses the he or she receives all the consequences listed.

The last teacher of the day sees that the student receives the negative or positive consequence.

Discipline Card

STUDENT_____ Date_____

Behaviors Teachers Expect:

Ex. <u>Hand in all assignments</u>

_____

_____

_____

CONSEQUENCES: **INITALS**

1st. (ex>) <u>Lunch detention</u>_____ _____

2nd. <u>15 minutes after school</u>_____ _____

3rd. _____ _____

4th. _____ _____

5th. _____ _____

POSITIVES:

<u>If none of the consequences are initialed after one week Susan is excused from one quiz.</u>

_____

COMMENTS:

SAMPLE U

GETTING TO KNOW YOU!

As it was discussed in Chapter Four, it is important to work with students so that bullying and poking fun at others is reduced to the bare minimum. The classroom teacher, consular, administration all working in harmony can reduce the potential for conflict with the school environment. Following are some "Activities" that might be used within the school setting to achieve the goal. The reduction of bullying, helping troubled kids, school shootings and the like.

GETTING TO KNOW YOU ACTIVITIES

INTEREST Inventory - Prepare an interview worksheet that will identify students' interests. "My favorite color, book, T.V. show, number, sport, game, etc. Have students search for others in class who may have a similar interest.

- Find a Friend; create a worksheet that allows students to get to know each other. Examples: Find a friend who... is an only child, Can operate a computer, Likes to eat spicy food, Can lay an instrument, and so on....

- The activity should consist of about 15-20 statements, enough for a wide range of interest and to make sure that no student is left out of the process.

- Allow students' enough time to interact with their classmates before beginning the activity. Once this interaction has occurred the student would begin the worksheet activity. It may be well to plan this activity in two settings to allow enough time for discussion and follow up between the individuals involved.

SAMPLE V

CLASS MEETING SAMPLES

1. **Agenda**
2. **Problem Solving**
3. **Lessons in Encouragement**
4. **Secretary's Binder**

CLASS MEETING AGENDA

While everyone is getting settled, empty out the box and read each paper. Separate information into problems or suggestions. Make sure the student know that if they do not sign the suggestions they will not be read.

1. CALL THE MEETING TO ORDER

2. ENCOURAGEMENT CIRCLE

- "Today, you will be encouraging me"
- Give a minute to think
- (Start with person beside you, go around circle).

3. OLD BUSINESS

- Ms ……… will now report on our old business
- "Thank you, Ms…

4. NEW BUSINESS

- (Empty out the Suggestion Box)
- Read out the problems first, then the suggestions
- See next page for help.

Ask Mis….. if there is time for thank-yours and compliments today.

5. CLOSE MEETING

- Thank everyone for listening and participating
- Say, "Please return to your seats quietly."

PROBLEM-SOLVING MODEL

    a) Each child has a copy in its Personal Planning notebook.
    b) Class Meeting Leader uses a copy for guidance during the meeting.

1. IDENTIFY THE PROBLEM
- "Can you tell us about the problem?"
- "What have you already done to try to solve this?"
- If another person(s) is involved, you now ask: "Is this true?"
- "Does anyone have any questions?"
- "What do you (person with problem) think would solve the problem?"
- Repeat this suggestion and ask the class, "Who thinks this might work?" Count hands. If it's a majority, problem is considered solved, if not, go on to next step.

2. BRAINSTORM POSSIBLE SOLUTIONS"
- What do you think would be a logical solution to this problem?"
- Secretary will record solutions.
- Go around the circle when asking for a response, taking hands up.
- People only get to speak once.
- Do not allow any discussion at this point, only solutions.

3. DISCUSS SOLUTIONS
- "Mrs. Styles would you please read the solutions."
- Ask the class for their opinions as to which solutions might work or not work and why.
- Allow discussion. If you see that the same ideas are being repeated, ask for an opposing point of view.

4. CHOOSE A SOLUTION
- "Ms_____ will read all the solutions.
- You can vote only once. Remember that a logical solution is the solution that you think would best solve the problem. And, it should be: - Respectful - Responsible - Related - Reasonable.
- Have Ms_____ read each one and count hands.

5. MAKE A PLAN
- If it involved a plan, figure out who will do what to make the solution happen.
- Ask if anyone has any advice for the person.
- If it is a suggestion that needs a committee, the person who puts the suggestion in can lead the committee if they wish. Choose an equal number of girls and boys to be on the committee and decide when they will meet (suggestion - keep the committee small).

A LESSON IN ENCOURAGEMENT

Adults often assume that children understand the meaning of a word and many times this is a false assumption. It is easier to achieve results when everyone involved has a common understanding of a word.

In order to have this common understanding about the meaning of the word "encouragement", hold a class discussion. The leader should ask the group, "What do you think the word encouragement means?" As the children tell their ideas, either the leader or another group member should record them on a chalkboard or large piece of paper. After all ideas are presented, the group should discuss them and come to a common agreement as to the meaning of the word.

Teach Children the Language of Encouragement

List the following ideas on a large piece of paper in language appropriate for the grade level being taught.

1. Encouragement is positive.
2. Encouragement is noticing improvement.
3. Encouragement is noticing when someone is trying hard.
4. Encouragement is noticing when someone is good at something.
5. Encouragements can begin with "I notice..." "I think..." "I like how..."

Each week, discuss with the class the meaning of one of these statements. Give examples of what each means and have the class practice the concept.

Donna Styles, Armstron

SAMPLE W

STUDENT CONSENT FORM

STUDENT CONCERN FORM	
Student: _____ Teacher: _____ Subject: _____	Date: _____ Current Mark: _____
In order that your son/daughter has a greater chance for success in this course, I would suggest special attention be paid to: _____ Regular attendance. # Absences _____ # Lates _____ _____ Improved attention and attitude in class. _____ Increased class participation. _____ Making a better attempt to follow teacher directions / instructions. _____ Prompt completion of all assignments / homework. _____ Improvement of study skills. _____ Other (please specify). _____ _____	
In order to obtain a satisfactory mark by the end of the semester he/she must: _____ _____	
_____ (Teacher's signature)	_____ (Parent's signature)
Parent's Comments	

SAMPLE X

DR PHIL'S ANTI BULLING PLEDGES

Anti-Bullying Pledge - Students

We the students of _____ agree to join together to stamp out bullying at our school.

We believe that everybody should enjoy our school equally, and feel safe, secure and accepted regardless of color, race, gender, popularity, athletic ability, intelligence, religion and nationality.

Bullying can be pushing, shoving, hitting, and spitting, as well as name calling, picking on, making fun of, laughing at, and excluding someone. Bullying causes pain and stress to victims and is never justified or excusable as "kids being kids," "just teasing" or any other rationalization. The victim is never responsible for being a target of bullying.

By signing this pledge, we the students agree to:

1. Value student differences and treat others with respect.
2. Not become involved in bullying incidents or be a bully.
3. Be aware of the school's policies and support system with regard to bullying.
4. Report honestly and immediately all incidents of bullying to a faculty member.
5. Be alert in places around the school where there is less adult supervision such as bathrooms, corridors, and stairwells.
6. Support students who have been or are subjected to bullying.
7. Talk to teachers and parents about concerns and issues regarding bullying.
8. Work with other students and faculty, to help the school deal with bullying effectively.

9. Encourage teachers to discuss bullying issues in the classroom.
10. Provide a good role model for younger students and support them if bullying occurs.
11. Participate fully and contribute to assemblies dealing with bullying.

I acknowledge that whether I am being a bully or see someone being bullied, if I don't report or stop the bullying, I am just as guilty.

Signed by: _____

Print name: _____

Anti-Bullying Pledge - Parents

We the parents of _____ agree to join together to stamp out bullying at our school.

We believe that everybody should enjoy our school equally, and feel safe, secure and accepted regardless of color, race, gender, popularity, athletic ability, intelligence, religion and nationality.

Bullying can be pushing, shoving, hitting, and spitting, as well as name calling, picking on, making fun of, laughing at, and excluding someone. Bullying causes pain and stress to victims and is never justified or excusable as "kids being kids," "just teasing" or any other rationalization. The victim is never responsible for being a target of bullying.

By signing this pledge, we the parents agree to:

1. Keep themselves and their children informed and aware of school bullying policies.

2. Work in partnership with the school to encourage positive behavior, valuing differences and promoting sensitivity to others.

3. Discuss regularly with their children their feelings about school work, friendships and relationships.

4. Inform faculty of changes in their children's behavior or circumstances at home that may change a child's behavior at school.

5. Alert faculty if any bullying has occurred.

Signed by: _____

Print name: _____

Date: _____

Anti-Bullying Pledge - Faculty

We the faculty of _____ agree to join together to stamp out bullying at our school.

We believe that everybody should enjoy our school equally, and feel safe, secure and accepted regardless of color, race, gender, popularity, athletic ability, intelligence, religion and nationality.

Bullying can be pushing, shoving, hitting, and spitting, as well as name calling, picking on, making fun of, laughing at, and excluding someone. Bullying causes pain and stress to victims and is never justified or excusable as "kids being kids," "just teasing" or any other rationalization. The victim is never responsible for being a target of bullying.

By signing this pledge, we the school and faculty agree to:

1. Develop a clear school policy on bullying and display it prominently in classrooms and around the school.
2. Train faculty in appropriate handling of incidents.
3. Develop or adopt a curriculum that educates students about bullying.
4. Teach students about less obvious forms of bullying like gossiping and exclusion.
5. Discuss pro-active anti-bullying measures (such as having lunch with a student who has been excluded in the past).
6. Establish support systems for pupils involved in incidents such as peer counseling and mediation.
7. Establish a system to support and inform parents when incidents of bullying occur.
8. Offer counseling to students who bully.
9. Ensure an atmosphere where students feel safe reporting incidents of bullying and confident they will be dealt with and not ignored.
10. Report all incidents of bullying immediately to the principal.
11. When an incident is reported all students involved will be given the opportunity to give their version of the incident.
12. Put in place sanctions for bullying such as verbal warnings, removal from a classroom or school grounds, a verbal or written apology to the victim, a parent teacher meeting, and detention or expulsion for repeat offenders.
13. Monitor cases of persistent of bullying and be fully informed of all incidents and their progress.

Signed by: _____

Print name: _____

Date: _____

Source : WWW.DrPhil.com February 27, 2003

Bullies February 27, 2003

Schoolyard bullying is far more serious than just name-calling and teasing. It's escalated to include harassment, beatings and even death threats.

What motivates children to bully? How can the victims of bullying fight back? What can students, parents and teachers do to eliminate bullies in their schools? Dr. Phil offers insight and advice, including how to launch an anti-bullying campaign in your school.

The Anti-Bullying Pledge

Dr. Phil encourages parents, students and teachers to launch anti-bullying campaigns in schools across the country, much like the one launched at the Barbara Bush Middle School.

Chapter Twelve

A WORKSHOP FOR PARENT'S AND PARENTAL INVOLVEMENT

COURSE PERFORMANCE OBJECTIVES

SCOPE AND SEQUENCE

The following objectives are divided into four separate workshops. Keep in mind that the term student is referring to the parent.

Workshop 1: Communications between home and school.

Final objective: After workshop one, the students will be able to practice effective communication between home and school through observing and participating in class activities

Week 1: The student will be able to prepare for an effective parent/teacher conference.

Week 2: The student will identify positive and negative ways of communication between home and school.

Week 3: The student will be able to validate the importance of effective communication.

Week 4: The student will demonstrate the importance of communication through role-playing.

Workshop 2: Parent as an Educator.

Final Objective: Without teacher guidance, the student will be able to transfer their knowledge of being a parent educator that was discussed in class to their home environment.

Week 5: The student will interpret their child's learning style.

Week 6: The student will identify at-risk children.

Week 7: The student will demonstrate ways of helping their child learn through hands-on class activities.

Week 8: The student will develop an activity to help their child learn concept that they are having difficulties with.

Workshop 3: Parent involvement through volunteering.

Final Objective: Without teacher guidance, the student will be able to discover ways in which they can become involve and volunteer at their child's school.

Week 9: The student will formulate ways of becoming involved with their Children's' school.

Week 10: The student will be able to recognize their own barriers of parent involvement.

Week 11: The student will be able to explain the importance of parent involvement through volunteering.

Week 12: The student will apply what they have learned in workshop 3 in their child's school.

Workshop 4: Educational activities for the summer months.

Final Objective: Through practiced activities in class, the students are able to construct and apply a list of summer activities to do with their children.

Week 13: The student will recognize the importance of academics in the summer months.

Week 14: The student will create a summer activity for their child.

Week 15: The student will illustrate a summer activity in class.

Week 16: The student will be able to select 10 summer activities that fit their child's learning style.

LESSON/ACTIVITY

Background Information: The students will have discussed the importance of summer activities to maintain the child's interest in learning. The students will have some prior knowledge on how to implement an academic activity with their own children. This lesson is designed to teach the parent how to instigate learning at home. The following activity will be apart of the workshop: Educational activities for the summer months.

Objective: Through practice of the activity, the student will be able to apply the lesson to suit his or her own child's age.

Materials: 1. Magazines, scissors, glue, paper, and markers.

2. Separate instructions for age group assigned.

Procedure/Activity: Following a discussion on the importance of academic learning through the summer break, parents will be asked to write down the amount of time they are in the home with the child.

Parents will then be asked to write down what kind of activities they do with their children during the duration that they are at home. Due to parent work schedules, the answers will vary.

Discussion and sharing of activities pertaining to the difficulties of work schedules that interfere with parent/child relations. How can they manage their time better?

Activity led by teacher:

Divide the class into groups according to the age of their children. Three groups will be established: ages 5-6, ages 7-9, and ages 10-11.

The entire class will be given the following directions:

1. One person in the group will be the parent.

2. The remaining students will take on the role of their own child's age.

3. The parent will be given instructions on paper of the activity that they need to engage their children in.

4. The person playing the role of the parent will read the directions silently and when finished

will do the activity with the students taking the role of the children.

Group 1 instructions – ages 5-6

1. Have the children find uppercase letters A, B, and C and lower case letters a, b, and c in the magazines. Have the child find different sizes, shapes, and script of the letters.
2. Cut and paste the letters on paper. Have the children practice writing the letters that they pasted.
3. Have the children find all the letters in their name and cut and paste them to their A, B, and C paper on the bottom.
4. Display work in the home and talk about how well they did.

Group 2 instructions –ages 7-9

1. Have the children find five different letter styles in the magazine: balloon, gothic, script, and cartoon. The children then will copy the letters onto a piece of paper. Have the children think of their own way to write a new style of letter.
2. Cut and paste each letter found in the magazine on a separate piece of paper.
3. Have the children draw an animal or object out of their own style of letter next to the letter they cut and pasted from the magazine.
4. Display artwork and talk to the children about what they did and what they liked about the activity.

Group 3 instructions – ages 10-11

1. Have the children cut out several words from the magazine.
2. Paste the words on a piece of paper to make a short story. Keep in mind that they need to have a subject and predicate part of each sentence.
3. They can draw a picture in place of a few words.
4. Display stories and have the children read it to his/her family. Congratulate the child for their creative story.

Discussion: When the activity is completed by all groups, each student with the role of the parent will be asked how they presented the activity and if they had any concerns about how they did. Other students may offer suggestions. Each student pretending to be the child will be asked if they clearly understood the activity and what could the parent have done to make the activity clearer.

Closure: Parents will write down any questions that they had about the activity in order to present it to their own children at home, due to the fact that every child is different. Questions will be answered in the same class period.

Homework: Do the same activity with their child at home and bring in the finished product. Discussion on how it went will take place in the next class period. Come up with one academic activity on your own that your child would be interested in.

LESSON/ACTIVITY

Background Information: The students have prior knowledge on parent/teacher conferences due to class lecture, materials, and discussion. The following lesson/activity will be included in the workshop: Communications between home and school.

Objective: Students will be able to prepare for an effective parent/teacher conference.

Materials: 1. Student scenarios

Procedure/Activity: Students will review the positive aspects of a parent/teacher conference such as: going in with a list of concerns, being open-minded, and have questions relating to student achievement.

Students will review the negative aspects of a conference, such as: poor attitude, rushing the speaker, and not sharing concerns.

Students will make a list of what to do before, during, and after a conference. Teacher will hand out a similar list adapted from a parent communication web site.(cnet.unb.ca/cap/partners/chsptt/conferences.html).

Students will get into groups of three. Each group will be handed a scenario. Some scenarios will be the same. They will role-play a parent/teacher conference. The students will decide the role of the three people; mother, father, teacher, principal, counselor, etc. (Scenarios attached).

Following the activity, students will point out the positive and negative aspects that took place in the mock conference. One group for each scenario will be chosen to present their conference. The teacher and the students will give feedback.

Closure: Students may ask questions about their own concerns with their child's teacher. Appropriate information on how to handle their particular situation will be given.

Homework: Study for quiz on parent/teacher communications

Scenarios

Scenario 1.: Your daughter is in first grade and is very intelligent. The teacher wants to move your child up a grade because she is capable of and will excel at the second grade level. As a parent you feel that socially your child is not ready to skip a grade. The teacher tells you that your child is bored in class and is a bit of a troublemaker because of this. You feel that the teacher is not cooperating with the way you feel about your own child.

1.) Should you bring in a third party?
2.) Do you give in to the teacher?
3.) How would you communicate with the teacher in the conference?
4.) What type of attitude would you exhibit?

Scenario 2.: (Taken from Parents as Partners in Education, 2000).

"I've never come to a school conference without having to wait 45 minutes to talk with you. Then, when I get in, you rush me, never let me ask questions, and just tell me how poorly Mary is doing. I know that Mary is doing poorly! I have my hands full just trying to go to work and feed my four children. Can't you do something to help Mary? Do you care?" Mary's father breathlessly expressed his anger and frustration.

"Hold on, Mr. Wimble," Mr. Bush said. "You're responsible for Mary, not me. She does poorly because she doesn't pay attention; she's more interested in her friends than in school, and she cuts class. I can work with students who come to school ready to learn. I just don't have the strength or the patience to take on you daughter until she changes her attitude."

"I waited 45 minutes to hear that?" Mr. Wimble asked. "What's going on here? No wonder Mary skips school. Where's the superintendent's office? I need to talk with you supervisor." Mr. Wimble stalked out of the room.

1. What kind of interaction should take place to promote problem solving?
2. What can Mr. Wimble do to help resolve his daughter's problem?
3. What responsibility does Mary have?
4. Going into the conference how should have Mr. Wimble responded to waiting 45 minutes?

5. When role-playing this scenario, change it to the way the conference should have been handled.

Scenario 3.: Your son's teacher has requested a conference with you. The teacher, Mrs. Bloom, is willing to meet with you in the morning, after school, or in the evening. She even suggested that if you can't find a sitter that she would have something for your child to do while the conference is taking place. It is at the end of the school year and your son, Pete, is failing math, reading, and science. He will not be promoted to the sixth grade unless he raises his grades. You work two jobs and feel that you don't have time for the conference but you know you have to go. Your husband just asked for a separation and took off. Therefore you will be attending the conference alone.

1. How will you prepare for the conference?
2. What concerns will you bring in to the conference?
3. What information will you offer the teacher about life at home?
4. What will you do to follow up on the conference?

LESSON/ACTIVITY

Background Information: The students/parents have knowledge on different ways to become involved in the school whether it be through volunteering in the classroom or out of the classroom. The students/parents will have been given handouts on how to become involved with their child's education. The following lesson will be included in the parent involvement through volunteering workshop.

Objective: Students will be able to formulate ways to become more involved with their children through self-understanding.

Materials: 1. Worksheets
2. Butcher paper, markers

Procedure/Activity:
1. Students will get into groups of four to complete brainstorming activity.
2. Instructions for brainstorming activity: students will brainstorm and write down their thoughts on what it is to Students will post their butcher paper on the wall.
3. Class will discuss the words in which they wrote down.
4. Students will come up with an analogy of their own on how they feel being a parent is like. For example, being a parent is like...
5. Students will share their analogies to be discussed.
6. Hand out worksheet for students to complete. After completed go over answers. (Attached)

Closure: Go over completed worksheets and discuss ideas in which the student can become involved in their child's school and education.

Homework: None

Learning to be a Better Parent
(From Coan, D.L., and Gotts, E.E. (1976). *Parent education needs: A national assessment study*)

Handout on following page.

EXAMPLE OF A LESSON/ACTIVITY

Background Information: This lesson is designed to fit in with the workshop on Parents as educators. The students will have prior knowledge on ways to improve their child's motivation towards learning. The students will also have discussed why teachers assign homework and why it is necessary. The following lesson focuses on homework issues.

Objective: The student will interpret their child's learning style as to help with the child's homework assignments.

Materials: 1. Handouts
2. Crayons, Pencils, Paper,
3. Apples, Knife
4. Story books

Procedure/Activity:
1. Short lecture on why it is important to understand a child's learning style and what the learning styles are.
2. Have the students write down what they think their child's learning style is.
3. Ask: What are the cons for doing your child's homework for them?
4. Pass out the "Checklist for Helping Your Child With Homework" (taken from **http://www.ed.gov/pubs/parents/Homework/pt10.html**)
5. Students will be placed into groups according to the learning style of their child. The groups will be divided into visual, audio, or kinesthetic learning. Groups should only consist of four people. There may be more than one group per learning style.

6. Instruct each group to do a lesson that fits their child's learning style. Separate instructions for each group are as follows:

Visual: Choose three people to be the student and one person to be the parent. These children learn concepts by seeing something that they need to learn. Explain the concept of learning about the difference between two similar animals. For example, the difference between a housecat and a tiger. After you verbally explain the difference, ask the student to explain it. After the students explain the difference, draw the two different animals on paper and see if they can remember the difference of the animals better.

Audio: Read the animal book to your student. Do not have the student write down any of the information. Following the story ask questions about what type of animals were in the book and what are the attributes of the animals in the book.

Kinesthetic: Explain to your students that you will be explaining fractions to them. Take an apple and cut it in half. Let the students pick up the apple to feel it. Then cut the apple in half again. Let the students pick up the apple and explain that if the apple is cut into four pieces each piece is $1/4^{th}$. Cut the apple again as many times as you would like to make more fractions. Each time you cut the apple let the student handle the pieces and see if they can put the pieces back together.

Closure: When the groups have finished the activity, come together as one group. Discuss any complications that they may have had. The teacher will then model each activity for the entire class. Discuss ways in which they can help their child with their homework problems.

Homework: Have the parents work with their child and their homework. Come in next week with an assignment that their child had problems with. Next class period the homework problems will be discussed and suggestions will be offered on how to help with each individual's homework problem.

LESSON/ACTIVITY

Background Information: The students will have discussed the importance of summer activities to maintain the child's interest in learning. The students will have some prior knowledge on how to implement an academic activity with their own children. This lesson is designed to teach the parent how to instigate learning at home. The following activity will be apart of the workshop: summer activities to continue the child's learning.

Objective: Through practice of the activity, the student will be able to apply the lesson to suit his or her own child's age.

Materials: 1. Magazines, scissors, glue, paper, and markers.
2. Separate instructions for age group assigned.

Procedure/Activity: Following a discussion on the importance of academic learning through the summer break, parents will be asked to write down the amount of time they are in the home with the child.

Parents will then be asked to write down what kind of activities they do with their children during the duration that they are at home. Due to parent work schedules, the answers will vary.

Discussion and sharing of activities pertaining to the difficulties of work schedules that interfere with parent/child relations. How can they manage their time better?

Activity led by teacher:

Divide the class into groups according to the age of their children. Three groups will be established: ages 5-6, ages 7-9, and ages 10-11.

The entire class will be given the following directions:
5. One person in the group will be the parent.
6. The remaining students will take on the role of their own child's age.
7. The parent will be given instructions on paper of the activity that they need to engage their children in.
8. The person playing the role of the parent will read the directions silently and when finished will do the activity with the students taking the role of the children.

Group 1 instructions – ages 5-6

5. Have the children find uppercase letters A, B, and C and lower case letters a, b, and c in the magazines. Have the child find different sizes, shapes, and script of the letters.

6. Cut and paste the letters on paper. Have the children practice writing the letters that they pasted.

7. Have the children find all the letters in their name and cut and paste them to their A, B, and C paper on the bottom.

8. Display work in the home and talk about how well they did.

Group 2 instructions – ages 7-9

5. Have the children find five different letter styles in the magazine: balloon, gothic, script, and cartoon. The children then will copy the letters onto a piece of paper. Have the children think of their own way to write a new style of letter.

6. Cut and paste each letter found in the magazine on a separate piece of paper.

7. Have the children draw an animal or object out of their own style of letter next to the letter they cut and pasted from the magazine.

8. Display artwork and talk to the children about what they did and what they liked about the activity.

Group 3 instructions – ages 10-11

5. Have the children cut out several words from the magazine.

6. Paste the words on a piece of paper to make a short story. Keep in mind that they need to have a subject and predicate part of each sentence.

7. They can draw a picture in place of a few words.

8. Display stories and have the children read it to his/her family. Congratulate the child for their creative story.

Discussion: when all groups complete the activity, each student with the role of the parent will be asked how they presented the activity and if they had any concerns about how they did. Other students may offer suggestions. Each student pretending to be the child will be asked if they clearly understood the activity and what could the parent have done to make the activity clearer.

Closure: Parents will write down any questions that they had about the activity in order to present it to their own children at home, due to the fact that every child is different. Questions will be answered in the same class period.

Homework: Do the same activity with their own child at home and bring in the finished product. Discussion on how it went will take place in the next class. Period. Come up with one academic activity on your own that your child would be interested in.

SUMMARY

Parental Involvement- Only a plus

If we as educators are truly concerned, which thee is no doubt that we are, about the safety of students not only for Themselves but for those around them we must look at the fact that the prime educators of children are their parents. This chapter provides some vital information and a means for parental involvement in the child's life. It focuses on the elementary grades but could easily be expended to the secondary school level.

Parental involvement at the secondary level could be in the form of a workshop design however students during their teen years would rather not have that close of an involvement between school and home. It is therefore the belief of the authors that the years that can lay the "ground work " and set the "foundation" are the pre-teen year's, those years when the student is at the elementary level, grades K - 6.

INTERNET INFORMATION.

What you do at home:

- Watch videos of how parents and children behave toward each other.
- Read articles on child psychology that pertain to the specific topic or issue.
- Answer workbook exercises designed to help you reflect upon the articles.
- Apply principles of effective parenting at home.

Reflect upon your new and old parenting methods

The Now and Future Parent Video Series:
Adapted for parents of children in preschool and elementary school

Available in English, Spanish, and French!

Parents are grouped according to children's age or similar situations.
- Increase your children's chances of success in school.
- Hear other parents' various and opposing viewpoints regarding best practices in parenting.
- Evaluate common situations you and your children face together.
- Read short articles in child psychology.
- Reflect upon your parenting techniques and write your thoughts in a personal journal.

In this class you will study:

1. Self-esteem
2. Discipline
3. Communication
4. Handling parental & child stress
5. Dealing with sibling rivalry and rivalry with other children

6. Teaching responsibility
7. Social development
8. Health & safety practices
9. Attitudes toward the importance of play
10. Kindergarten readiness (only for parents of children ages 3 to 6)

Understanding Your Teenager:

Adapted for parents of middle school or high school children

The early teenage years are filled with wonder and mystery. You will examine pre-teen and teenage behavior, from normal developmental issues to difficulties that require serious intervention.

- Conflict, Rebellion & Resolution
- Communicating with Teens
- Encouraging Your Child
- Family Dynamics
- Setting Limits
- Physical Development
- Teen Parents
- Social Development
- Self-Esteem
- Living in and among Divorced and Blended Families

SARAH ROBINSON

Parents' involvement key to good schools

September 1, 2002 1:02 amWASHINGTON--There has been a lot of heat- ed talk lately, much of it coming from pundits and politicians, suggesting that public-school parents are "consumers" who deserve "a better buy" for their money.

I find this offensive. Calling school parents "consumers" is like referring to the Grand Canyon as "landscape." It does not begin to tell the whole story.

What annoys me most is the implication that a proper role for parents in the schools is passive, detached, complaining from the sideline like disgruntled sports fans helpless to influence the real action. That is not just wrong; it's dangerous.

This fall more than 53 million children begin a new academic year in the nation's public schools and there may be no greater factor in how they perform--and how the schools perform--than the role of their parents. And I am not just talking about the obvious benefits in helping kids with homework (though not, I caution, doing it for them!).

In my experience, parental involvement is every bit as important as the headline-grabbing issues of vouchers, testing, and standards. But parents beware: Like any travel on a crucial mission, you must learn to navigate the complex pathways or risk getting lost.

Educators, regrettably, are not very good at posting road signs and issuing user manuals. We do not set out to baffle parents, but too often that is what happens. Parents must realize that critical areas of their child's schooling are, in fact, accessible. For example:

Teacher quality. Nearly all parents consider this to be the most important element in a child's education--and rightly so. Most teachers have a lot to offer. It is important for parents to orient their child to a positive and productive attitude and to really talk with their child's teacher. Find out what your child is expected to learn this year. And if the teacher slips into jargon, so-called "eduspeak," you have every right to request plain English, please.

Lack of challenge in the classroom. Parents can learn how to tell when "I'm bored" is a legitimate complaint, how to talk with the teacher about it, and what remedies the school ought to have in its repertoire.

Falling behind. Parents can also learn how to tell if the slippage is serious, what additional testing may be called for, how the child study team functions, and what strategies the classroom teacher can use.

These are not secrets. Learning them, however, requires dialoguing with staff and other parents, attending school functions, reading up, exploring, and participating.

Schools need to do a better job of explaining themselves to parents, and not simply as a feel-good exercise. A Department of Education study found that reading and math scores of low-achieving students rose 40 percent to 50 percent when teachers reached out to families throughout the school year--not just when the child was in trouble.

Wishing it, of course, does not make it so. Parents these days are horribly squeezed for time. Employers must do more to accommodate parents who want to be actively engaged in their child's education, and schools must find ways to open themselves to parents with busy lives. What's more, school systems must reduce class sizes, especially in the early grades, so that teachers can devote more individual attention to your child and you.

Families who understand how schools work is vastly better equipped to help their children, and the payoff goes both ways. Savvy families tend to be the strongest supporters of schools. Why? Because by gaining "school smarts," parents learn a very basic lesson. Namely, schools are a living, breathing community in which adults come together to do what's best for the children. And parents are that community's nerve system.

This fall, as students pass eagerly, or apprehensively, through the schoolhouse doorway, millions of concerned parents face an urgent choice, a test as important as any their child will take this school year: a) to be a passive consumer or; b) to be a contributing member of a vibrant community that just happens to hold the key to your child's future.

It shouldn't be hard to get that one right.

BOB CHASE is author of "The New Public School Parent: How to Get the Best Education for Your Child" and is the outgoing two-term president of the National Education Association.

Copyright 2001 The Free Lance-Star Publishing Company.
Northwest Life: Saturday, September 07, 2002

Families

How teachers can get parents more involved Here are some ways parents say teachers could help them stay involved in their child's **education**.

Ask for parental help more than once and offer suggestions on how.

"Parents want more meaningful ways to be involved besides copying and stapling," said Laura Bay, a mom of a 12-, 14- and 16-year-old who also teaches a fourth-and-fifth-grade class in Bremerton.

Teachers can help by giving specific examples of what they need parents to do, or letting families know general topics of study and asking if parents can offer any expertise.

At the secondary-school level, many kids don't want parents in their classes on a regular basis. However, sometimes parents can help out in other areas such as the library or main office and learn a lot just by listening to other students.

A one-time or occasional project, such as helping with a science-class lab, gives parents a chance to visit the school and not feel like they're intruding, said Susan Fyall of Kenmore, a former high-school English teacher who teaches classes on how parents can navigate the secondary-school system to PTAs.

Update Web Sites.

Notes have a way of getting lost or misplaced, which is why several parents asked if teachers could keep Web sites updated with major-assignment guidelines and deadlines. This is especially important in middle and high school when students responsible for writing down assignments might miss a key requirement.

While parents don't expect a detailed list of what's studied every day, Bay requested a general overview of the main subjects so she knows what topics to reinforce at home. It also helps with reticent kids to know what sorts of questions to ask about what they're studying, she noted.

Give parents more notice if children aren't doing well.

Schools try to do this with midterm reports, but in most cases, by the time they're mailed out and received, there's only a month left in the grading term, Fyall said.

"It has to be early enough to make a difference," said the mother of two, the younger of whom is a high-school senior. "Too often, by the time midterm reports arrive, the fate of the grade is sealed."

She also wishes teachers were more frank with parents when students aren't working up to their potential, even if they're getting a decent grade.

"Some teachers don't like to say, 'I think he could be doing better,' " said Fyall. "But if parents get more honest feedback, they might help improve the student's performance."

Older students are easily embarrassed and not eager to raise their hands and say, "I don't get it," Fyall said. "A lot can happen before kids get help."

Don't send home nothing.

If a homework folder comes home empty or a planner doesn't have anything written in it, should parents assume there truly isn't anything required — or their child forgot it?

"I'll notice there's nothing on their planner for a week, so I'll write a note asking the teacher if they're missing something," Bay said. "I get frustrated when I don't hear anything back. The teacher could just sign their initials to acknowledge that, yes, the child is using the planner correctly."

Give parents feedback on more than just grades.

On progress reports, teachers often have space for extra notes but sometimes don't take the time. When they do, it helps parents get a sense of how kids are doing in class beyond the simple letter grades.

"I know my son tends to talk too much," Fyall said. "I know he tries not to. If he's not trying hard enough, I want to know."

Come to parent gatherings such as PTA meetings or open houses.

"It's great when parents can talk to teachers in a casual circumstance," Fyall said. "Parents can learn so much about what's going on generally. They might not be able to tell me about my child specifically, but I can learn what's expected overall."

Don't schedule major projects or assignments over long weekends and vacations.

Just as teachers feel parents should make **education** a priority, parents believe teachers should respect the importance of family time. Many families like to travel over long weekends or vacations and major homework commitments cut into time kids can spend with parents and relatives.

Copyright © 2002 The Seattle Times Company

Target: Elementary, Middle, Senior High Administrators and Department.

Duration: 1-3 days.

Create a culture of peace in your school where students grow intellectually, socially, and spiritually within a community of respect and understanding. The aim of the culture of peace is the involvement of everyone (students, faculty, cafeteria and other support personnel, parents) working together towards a common goal.

All participants will receive materials suitable for their grade level and become part of the Peace Education Network which offers on-going support and trouble shooting. All workshops and seminars will be tailored to the needs and experiences of participants and are offered on or off-site.

The State of Iowa has an excellent program for parents and can be obtained at:

Iowa Department of Education
Grimes State Office Building
Des Moines, Iowa 50319-0146
Phone: 515/281-5294
Fax: 515/242-5988
URL: http://www.state.ia.us/educate/

Source:
State of Iowa
Department of Education
Grimes State Office Building
Des Moines, Iowa 50319-0146

- Chapter 1: The Basics of Parent and Family Involvement
- Chapter 2: Getting Parents' Point of View
- Chapter 3: Two-Way Communication between Home and School
- Chapter 4: Involving Parents in the Life of the School
- Chapter 5: Parent Involvement in Preschool
- Chapter 6: Joint Home-School Learning Activities
- Chapter 7: Parent Education Activities and Workshops
- Chapter 8: Organizations Providing Parent and Family Involvement

REFERENCES FOR PARENTS

Clark, R. (1988). Parents as providers of linguistic and social capital. *Educational Horizons*, 66(2), 93-95.

Clark, R. (1990). Why disadvantaged students succeed. *Public Welfare* (Spring) : 17-23.

Cooper, H. (1989). *Homework*. New York: Longmen.

Epstein, J. (1984). Paths to partnership: What can we learn from federal, state, district, and school initiatives? *Phi Delta Kappan*, 72, 344-349.

Epstein, J. (1991). Effects of student achievement of teacher practices on parent involvement. in S. Silvern (ed.). *Advances in Reading Language Research*, Vol. 5, Literacy through family, community and school interaction. Greenwich, CT: JAI Press.

Mayeske, G.W. (1973). *A study of achievement of our nation's students*. Washington, DC: U.S. Department of Health, Education and Welfare. (ERIC Document Reproduction Service No. ED 102 666).

Scott-Jones, D. (1984). Family influence on cognitive development and school achievement. *Review of Research in Education*, 11, 259-304.

Walbert, H.J., Paschal, R.A., & Weinstein, T. (1985). Homework's powerful effects of learning. *Educational Leadership*, 42(7), 76-79.

BIBLIOGRAPHY

Baker, Amy (2000). Making the Promise of Parent Involvement a Reality. *The High School Magazine*, January 2000, Volume 7, Number 5, pp. 14-17.

Becker, Wesl y C., <u>Parents are Teachers,</u> Research Press, Champaign, IL., C. 1979.

Brenna, Susan (2000). The Cheater's Guide to School Volunteering. *Family Life*, December 2000, pp75-79.

Carey, N., Farris, E., & Westat. Inc.(1996). Parents and Schools: Partners in Student Learning. *National Center for Education Statistics*, October 1996.

Charles, C. M., <u>Building Classroom Discipline: From Models to Practice,</u> Longham, New York, NY. c. 1985.

Coopersmith, Stanley, <u>The antecedents of self-esteem,</u> W. H. Freeman, San Francisco, CA, c. 1967.

Guttman, Monika (1995). Beyond the Bake Sale. *America's Agenda*, Spring, 1995, pp. 12-19.

Dobson, James, - <u>Dare to Discipline,</u> Tyndale House Publishers, Weaton, IL, c. 1973.

Dodd, Anne, and Konzal, Jean (2000). Parents and Educators as Partners. *The High School Magazine*, January 2000, Volume 7, Number 5, pp. 8-13.

Donna Styles, Armstrong, B.C. The World Wide Web., June, 2001.

Fried, Hilda, National Institute of Mental Health, Division of Scientific and Public Information, (Plain Talk Series), Rockville, Md.

Hurlock, Elizabeth, Guidepost for Growing Up. : Standard Educational Corporation: Chicago, IL, c. 1972

Karlin, Muriel and Berger, Regina, Discipline and the Disruptive Child: A Practical Guide for Elementary Teachers. Parker Publishing Co. West Nyack, NY. c. 1972.

Mayer, Barbara, The High School Survival Guide : VGM Career Horizons, Skokie, IL c. 1982.

Meadows, B.J. (1993). Through the Eyes of Parents. *Educational Leadership*, October 1993, pp.31-33.

Nelson, Jane, Ed.D. Positive Discipline, Ballantine Bookc, New

York, NY, c. 1981. Seeley, David (1989). A New Paradigm for Parent Involvement. *Educational Leadership* October 1989, pp. 46-48.

Ziegler, William (2000). Venturing Beyond the Schoolyard to Bring Parents In. *The High School Magazine*, January 2000, Volume 7, Number 5, pp. 22-25.